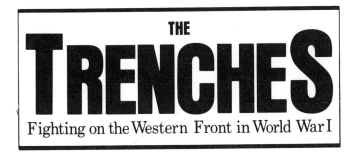

THE TRENCHES

Fighting on the Western Front in World War I

ABOUT THE BOOK

It was known as the Great War and it has been called the end of an age of innocence. The young who marched off to fight in it expected a war of great adventure and an opportunity for personal heroism. But, as Dorothy and Thomas Hoobler point out in this fascinating book, the young idealists were doomed to disappointment.

By the end of 1914, a gigantic gash had been scratched across the face of Europe from the North Sea to the Alps. Two opposing lines of trenches had been dug, and crouching inside them were the armies of England, France, and Germany facing each other in deadly combat. They would remain there for more than three years. These soldiers, rather than finding glory in war, died by the hundreds of thousands in senseless battles while the survivors lived like rats in filth and mud from day to day.

With a realism not for the squeamish, Mr. and Mrs. Hoobler tell as rarely has been done before the nightmare of living and dying on the Western Front in World War I. Extraordinary photographs, many never published before, illustrate their vivid words.

THE TRENCHES

Fighting on the Western Front in World War I

BY DOROTHY AND THOMAS HOOBLER

G.P. Putnam's Sons New York

Library of Congress Cataloging in Publication Data
Hoobler, Dorothy.
  The trenches.

  Bibliography: p. 180
  Includes index.
  SUMMARY: Describes the combat experiences of English,
French, and German soldiers on the Western Front during the Great
War.
  1. European War, 1914–1918—Campaigns—Western—Juvenile
literature. [1. World War I, 1914–1918—Campaigns—
Western] I. Hoobler, Thomas, joint author. II. Title.
D530.H66 1978   940.4'144   78-2698
ISBN 0-399-20640-X

Third Impression

CONTENTS

As the declarations of war rang out in the capitals of Europe in the summer of 1914, the mood was one of elation. Crowds along the Wilhelmstrasse in Berlin and the Champs Elysées in Paris bestowed flowers and kisses on the departing soldiers. Shouts of "On to Paris!" or "On to Berlin!" filled the air. The German ruler, Kaiser Wilhelm, spoke proudly of his country's unity in saying, "No more parties, Germans all!" Similar sentiments were echoed in other countries.

The young men who marched off to war swelled with feelings of pride and patriotism. They expected the war to be a great adventure and an opportunity for personal heroism. Rupert Brooke, who was to die in the war, expressed the feelings of many: "Now God be thanked who has matched us with His hour,/ And caught our youth, and wakened us from sleeping."

The enthusiasm for the war in 1914 included the expectation that it would be a short one. The Kaiser promised his soldiers that they would be home "before the leaves fall." The British and French thought the war would be over by Christmas.

But by the end of 1914, a gigantic gash had been scratched across the face of Europe. From the North Sea to the Alps, two opposing lines of trenches had been dug. Crouching inside them were the armies of England, France, and Germany facing each other in deadly combat. They would remain there for more than three years. Rather than experiencing the glories of war,

1914　　　　　　　　　　　　**1**

the soldiers endured a molelike existence that held nothing but misery on a scale not imagined before the war.

The nineteenth century had seen the growth of armies of unprecedented size. Germany and France used universal conscription to build the largest armies the world had ever seen. Germany could call upon 5 million trained men; the French slightly less.

As the European armies grew, changes were made in their organization. One was the development of three distinct kinds of personnel: combat units, service units, and command. The combat units consisted of the traditional elements of infantry, artillery, and cavalry. But there was a great increase in the use of support troops assisted by modern technology. Communications and engineering forces were to work closely with front-line combat troops. Supply and medical corps increased in importance.

The role of command staffs also expanded. Modern warfare required headquarters at a safe distance from the battlefield to direct the operations of the mass armies that fought the war.

The armies were organized to allow the generals to make effective use of their huge military forces. The army was the largest military unit. Each nation organized armies of different sizes for different tasks. Each army was composed of corps, which were flexible in their size and type of personnel. Corps consisted of a number of divisions, which included combat units —infantry, artillery, cavalry—as well as support units. Corps had extra artillery, cavalry, and support troops to beef up divisions where they were needed.

The division was the basic unit of the army for fighting large actions. At full strength, divisions contained from twelve thousand to twenty thousand men. Each division was subdivided into brigades, brigades into regiments, regiments into battal-

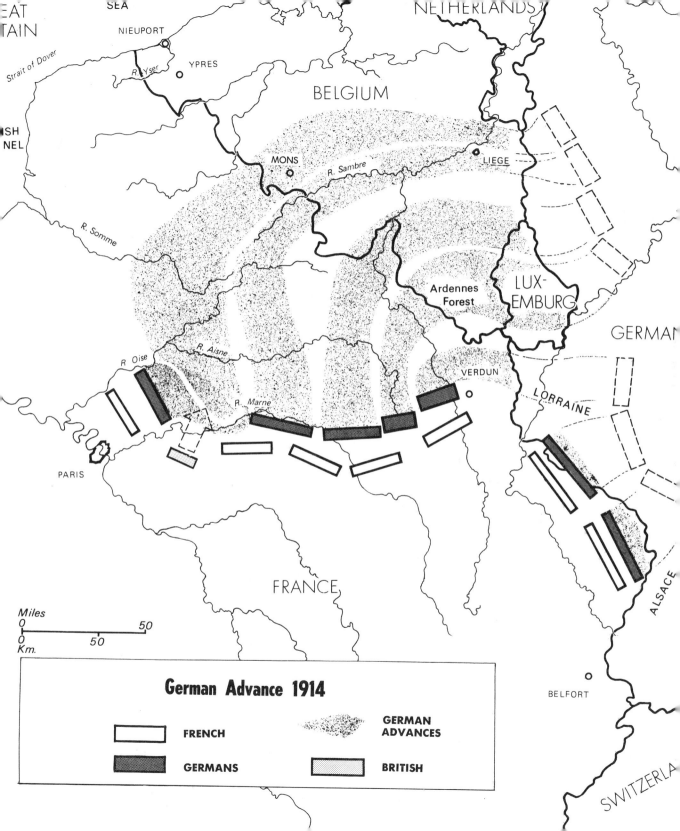

GREAT
BRITAIN

SEA

NIEUPORT

Strait of Dover

YPRES

R. Yser

ISH
NEL

NETHERLANDS

BELGIUM

MONS

R. Sambre

LIEGE

R. Somme

Ardennes
Forest

LUX-
EMBURG

GERMAN

R. Oise

R. Aisne

VERDUN

LORRAINE

R. Marne

PARIS

ALSACE

FRANCE

Miles
0   50
0   50
Km.

BELFORT

SWITZERLA

German Advance 1914

FRENCH

GERMAN
ADVANCES

GERMANS

BRITISH

ions, battalions into companies. Companies, the smallest units to be commanded by an officer, were divided into platoons, platoons into sections, and sections into groups.

The British had a small professional army in 1914. It was organized like the French and German armies, so that it was able to effectively use large numbers of volunteers and conscripts later in the war.

Developments in weaponry and transportation also changed the nature of modern warfare. But the generals were not experienced in the use of the new technology. They expected it to favor an all-powerful offensive thrust. Instead, it strengthened the defense, leading to the stalemate of trench warfare.

Both sides had prepared for a swift mobilization of troops. The men were assembled, equipped, and moved quickly to the battlefields by railroad. Mobilization had to move according to a strict timetable. Each side had drawn up careful plans of mobilization and attack that went into effect immediately on the outbreak of war.

The most important war plan was that of Germany. Called the Schlieffen Plan after the chief of staff who devised it, it was adopted with modifications by the current German Chief of Staff, Helmuth von Moltke. The plan was designed to enable Germany to avoid fighting on two fronts simultaneously. France, to the west of Germany, and Russia, to the east, were both allied and potential enemies. The Schlieffen Plan called for a six-week campaign against France. Then Germany would turn to defeat Russia, which because of its technological backwardness would be slow mobilizing.

Because of the importance of speed, Schlieffen's strategy was to avoid the heavily defended string of French forts from Belfort to Verdun and the Ardennes Forest. Germany would attack by sending the greater part of its forces through neutral

Belgium and Luxembourg. The German armies would come into France from the north and swing around like a wheel to the rear of the French armies.

Two small German armies at the French border would engage the French armies. They were to allow themselves to be driven slowly back into Germany so that the "strong right wing" coming around through Belgium would be able to catch the French in a pincer movement.

The French had their own plan, called Plan XVII. In the event of war, the French intended to attack across the Franco-German border and recapture the territories of Alsace and Lorraine, which had been lost in 1871. Plan XVII placed all its emphasis on a strong offensive.

The doctrine of the offensive was deeply ingrained in French military thinking. Springing from this was the belief in *élan*, or spirit, as a motivating force for the troops. The French generals truly believed that an attack with *élan* could overcome superiority in manpower, weaponry, and supply. Colonel Loiseau de Grandmaison, chief of operations of the French army in the years before the war, was influential in shaping this line of thought. He said: "For the attack only two things are necessary: to know where the enemy is and to decide what to do. What the enemy intends to do is of no consequence." French officers were often denied promotion for being too concerned about defense.

To launch the attack five French armies were assigned to the Alsace-Lorraine frontier. The French also counted on British help. In 1911, secret Franco-British talks had produced an agreement whereby Britain would send 100,000 men to fight on the left of the French armies, in case of invasion.

War broke out over an incident far from the French and German border. On June 28, 1914, the Austrian archduke Franz

Ferdinand was assassinated at Sarajevo in the Austrian province of Bosnia. Austria-Hungary made demands on Serbia for encouraging the assassins. The German Kaiser Wilhelm promised to support Austria. When Serbia failed to satisfy the Austrian demands, Austria-Hungary declared war. Russia responded in support of Serbia and began mobilizing for war. Germany ordered Russia to stop, and when the demand was ignored, Germany declared war on Russia on August 1. On August 3, Germany declared war on France, Russia's ally, and the next day England came into the war.

On August 3 German troops moved into Belgium. Their first obstacle was the city of Liège, surrounded by Belgian forts. The German Second Army, commanded by General Karl von Bülow, failed in its first attempt to cross the river that ran before Liège. After night fell, a hitherto little-known German colonel named Erich Ludendorff led a brigade of men through the circle of forts surrounding the city. On August 7 Liège fell, but the outer forts refused to surrender. The next day, the Germans brought up their 420-millimeter (16.5-inch) siege howitzers, called "Big Berthas." Despite a tenacious defense led by the Belgian General Gerard Leman, the forts were bombarded into submission. The forts, with thick walls to protect against cannon fire, were not prepared for shells falling from the high angle at which the howitzers fired.

The Germans swept onward, keeping to the timetable of the Schlieffen Plan, although Belgian resistance fighters harassed the German troops. Civilians suspected of sabotaging the German advance were rounded up and shot. The Germans also burned and looted captured towns. News of German brutality reached the outside world, embellished by exaggerated stories of atrocities. World opinion hardened against the German "rape of Belgium."

Meanwhile, the French had put Plan XVII into action. To lend *élan* to the attack, the French soldiers were dressed in colorful blue coats with bright red trousers and caps. They made perfect targets for German sharpshooters and machine gunners as they advanced in ranks across the border. Even though the French had numerical superiority, the Germans repulsed their attack. Farther north at the Ardennes Forest and the Sambre River, French attacks also met with failure. The early French battles cost them 300,000 casualties, testimony to the inadequacy of the doctrine of attack.

The British Expeditionary Force (BEF), led by Sir John French, had arrived on the Continent. Though few in number, the British troops were professional soldiers, probably man for man the best fighting force in Europe. At the Belgian city of Mons, British expert riflemen fired with such speed and accuracy that the Germans thought they were machine gunners. The German First Army was stopped.

But the British could not hold their position. The French army to the right of the British, under General Charles Lanrezac, had been forced to retreat by von Bülow's Second Army. When Sir John French learned of Lanrezac's retreat, he ordered his forces to fall back to protect their right flank.

The commander in chief of the French armies, General Joseph Joffre, realized he had underestimated the strength of the German army. Furthermore, Joffre now saw, the bulk of the German forces was much farther to the west than had been anticipated. Joffre began to rearrange his forces, taking troops from the Franco-German border to strengthen his left wing.

Joffre was a stubborn man, and clung tenaciously to the French doctrine of the offensive. He had one fine quality, however. He didn't panic easily. Despite the fact that his armies and the BEF were being pushed southward into France by the

German right wing, Joffre managed to keep his forces intact. The retreat was carried out skillfully to buy time as Joffre shifted his front.

While the French maneuvered, the German commander in chief, von Moltke, fretted. He kept receiving news of great German victories. But von Moltke asked, "Where are the prisoners? Where are the captured guns?" Though the Germans had advanced a long way, they had not succeeded in destroying the French armies. Joffre's retreat had withheld decisive victory from Germany.

Meanwhile, the French government in Paris was alarmed. The German First Army was drawing nearer to Paris. On September 2, the government fled to Bordeaux. The defense of Paris was left to soldiers under the command of General Joseph Galliéni. He rallied the citizens of Paris and organized his forces for the siege of the city that seemed imminent.

Then Galliéni's headquarters received news from a British scout who had flown over General von Kluck's army north of Paris. The Germans had turned and were now advancing on a line that would carry them east of the city. The flank of von Kluck's army was open to attack from the troops headquartered in Paris.

Von Kluck had turned to close a gap between his army and von Bülow's. During the long German march, lines of communication had become extended and strained. At headquarters, von Moltke was having trouble coordinating the march of his vast forces.

Galliéni persuaded Joffre to authorize an attack from Paris. Using twelve hundred Paris taxicabs as transport, Galliéni rushed every available man to join battle with the Germans at the river Marne. The fighting that followed is known as the Battle of the Marne.

French troops rushing northward to reinforce the French forces at the Marne. FRENCH EMBASSY PRESS AND INFORMATION DIVISION, NEW YORK

All along the front from Paris to Verdun, Joffre's armies turned to face the Germans. In a series of clashes from September 5 to 12, the French halted the German advance. Around Paris, von Kluck's army had turned back to face Galliéni's forces, and the gap between the German First and Second Armies widened. The British attacked at the vulnerable spot, and the Germans fell back to the Aisne River. "The miracle of the Marne," as the French call it, had saved France.

The French and British advanced to the Aisne, hoping to drive the Germans back to Germany, but they found the German troops entrenched in strong defensive positions, which the Germans held easily against Allied attacks.

Earlier at the Alsace-Lorraine border, the Germans counterattacked against French forces, who were falling back from their original defeats. The French dug in, linking up the forts guarding the border with primitive trench systems. The German attacks on the French fortifications were unsuccessful. As a result, the Germans began to construct their own trench lines opposite the French ones. From these beginnings, trench warfare developed.

After the deadlock at the Aisne, each side tried to envelop the other by moving swiftly around the flank of the opposing army. The only flank open was on the northwest side of the lines. Each army moved northwest, leaving behind a line of defensive trenches to keep the opposing side from breaking through.

Inexorably a line of trenches snaked its way from the Aisne across France and through Belgium until it reached the sea near the Belgian port of Nieuport. Neither army's flank had been turned, and now the opposing armies faced each other along a line from the sea to Switzerland.

General Erich von Falkenhayn had replaced von Moltke after the defeat at the Marne. Falkenhayn made the crucial decision to heavily fortify the German trenches. His men were fighting on enemy soil and he meant to hold the territory the Germans had won. German engineers were brought up to reinforce sections of the line. Machine-gun emplacements were constructed as strongpoints.

The first major attempt to break through the trench lines was at the First Battle of Ypres. Ypres, a small Belgian city, was to be the site of four major battles during the war. More than a million men would lose their lives there without any real advantage to either side. A "salient," or bulge, in the trench lines around Ypres was held jointly by the French and British. The Germans picked Ypres for attack because of its importance as a railway and communications center, and also because the Allied salient was open to attack on three sides.

On October 12, the Germans attacked. The cream of the British army held them back with accurate rifle fire. To the north of the salient, French and Belgian units gave way and were driven back to the Yser River. King Albert of the Belgians ordered dikes in the area to be opened, flooding the position and keeping the Germans from advancing farther.

After an Allied counterattack, the Germans renewed their offensive. Heavy bombardment by German artillery cut the Allied line to pieces. On October 29, the Germans, with a six to one superiority in numbers, swarmed over the Allied positions. The Allies threw in every available man to close the line. Finally, on November 12, snow began to fall and the battle sputtered out.

The British had lost more than fifty thousand men—half the BEF. German casualties were at least twice that many, and the French had lost nearly sixty thousand. The general staffs studied the enormous casualty lists in dismay. Two hundred thousand men lost without gain to either side. This was beyond anyone's expectations. No one knew as yet that the futile carnage was part of a pattern that would continue throughout the war.

At the end of 1914, the trenches in Western Europe extended more than 475 miles from the North Sea to the Alps. The first trenches were little more than foxholes dug for cover from enemy fire. Soon trench lines connecting the foxholes were dug, and the lines deepened so that a man could walk upright without exposing himself to enemy fire.

Falkenhayn's decision to reinforce the trenches was crucial in making them become permanent fixtures. The stronger their defenses, the less chance there was of a successful attack overrunning them.

On the other hand, the British and French were at first reluctant to heavily fortify their trenches. Their immediate goal was to drive the Germans back. The Allied generals felt that making the trenches too secure would lead to complacency among the troops and sap their will to attack. From the viewpoint of a British soldier:

> The whole conduct of our trench warfare seemed to be that we were not stopping in the trenches for long, but were tarrying a while on the way to Berlin. The result, in the long term, meant that we lived a mean and impoverished sort of existence in lousy scratch holes.

The trench resembled an "S" on its side as it ran through

THE BUILDING OF THE TRENCHES

2

Belgium and France over many kinds of terrain. The northern-most portion, from Nieuport on the North Sea down along the line of the Yser River and around the Ypres salient, was known as Flanders. Here the land was marshy and often flooded. The water table began about eighteen inches below the surface. The Germans held what little high ground there was in the area, including the Wytschaete-Messines Ridge, to be the site of a bloody battle.

South from the French town of Armentières, below Ypres, the trenches ran down through the industrial and mining area of Artois. Slag heaps dominated the generally flat landscape and made good positions for machine guns or observation posts.

As the trench line crept south of the city of Lens, the countryside became rolling chalk ridges. The first of these was Vimy Ridge, which would give its name to another bloody battle. This type of country, in which digging was arduous work, extended through Arras to the Somme River valley, where the ground became marshy again.

Near Noyon the line turned eastward, following the Aisne River to form the middle part of the "S." The Germans held the high ground north of the river, called the Chemin des Dames Ridge. French attacks on the Chemin des Dames would be costly.

The line crossed the river and ran southeast to the city of Reims. Between Reims and Verdun, the trenches stretched eastward through rocky, chalky terrain. Along the way the line rose through a rugged wooded highland known as the Argonne Forest. East of Verdun, the line turned south again to the Vosges Mountains and across the Belfort Gap to where it met the Swiss border.

Late in 1914, most of the northern part of the line, from Ypres to La Bassée in France, was held by the British. A small

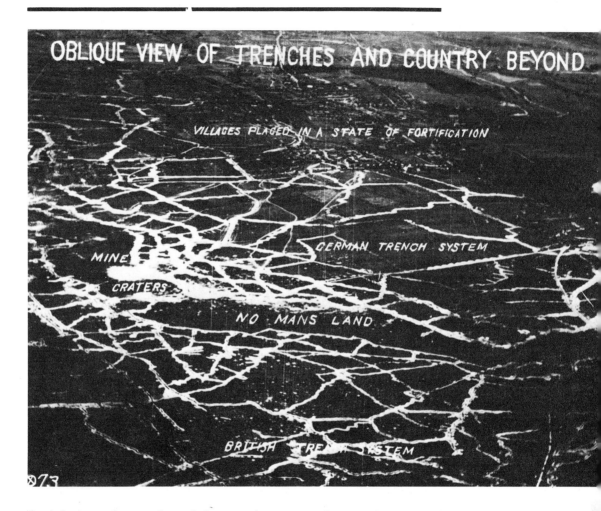

OBLIQUE VIEW OF TRENCHES AND COUNTRY BEYOND

VILLAGES PLACED IN A STATE OF FORTIFICATION

GERMAN TRENCH SYSTEM

MINE

CRATERS

NO MANS LAND

BRITISH TRENCH SYSTEM

Aerial view of a portion of the trench system, showing British and German trenches with no man's land in the middle. The picture was taken after the trench systems became highly developed. Building of the trenches continued throughout the war. NATIONAL ARCHIVES

contingent of Belgian troops held the area from Ypres to the sea. The French held the rest of the Allied line, from La Bassée to Switzerland. As the war went on, the British army expanded from 100,000 troops on the western front to over 2 million and their part of the line extended southward to the Somme region.

A typical British trench was divided into sections about ten yards in length, called "fire bays." The fire bays were separated from each other by walls of earth or sandbags. These barriers, called "traverses," extended out from the front wall of the trench at right angles, yet left space at the rear for a man to move from one firebay to the next. The purpose of the traverses was to prevent an enemy who captured a section of the trench from firing down the trench line and mowing down defenders. This tactic of raking an enclosed space with rapid fire was known as "enfilading fire." Other kinds of barriers, made of logs or piled-up debris, served as traverses in trenches constructed hastily under attack. From the air, the trench line broken up by traverses resembled a crenellated castle wall.

Trenches usually were seven or eight feet deep and about six feet wide, but they varied greatly in size. The front wall of the trench was called the "parapet," and the back wall, the "parados." Revetments made of sandbags, logs, or bundles of twigs and branches were used as supports for the trench walls.

Coverings of branches or cloth were used overhead to prevent enemy snipers from seeing the men in the trenches. Trench coverings were also made of wooden planks or metal in an attempt to shield the occupants from shrapnel and shell fire.

On the front wall, or parapet, was a ridge called the "fire step." When men stood sentry duty or the soldiers had to "stand to" to be on guard for attacks, they stood on this fire step to see over the top of the trench. Normally there were sandbags

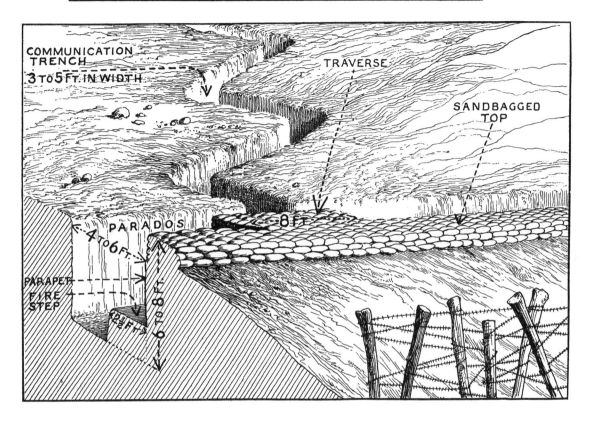

Diagram showing a typical British front-line and communication trench. Because of different conditions in the terrain, the types of trench varied from region to region. ARTHUR GUY EMPEY, OVER THE TOP, G.P. PUTNAM'S SONS, © 1917, BY ARTHUR GUY EMPEY

27

French soldiers repairing the damage done to their trenches in a recent attack. This kind of work was continuous. Artillery bombardment and bad weather also made frequent repairs necessary. NATIONAL ARCHIVES

on top of the parapet to shield men standing on the fire step. A narrow space left in these sandbags to allow the men to fire through was called an "embrasure."

In the marshy areas of the front it was impossible to dig deep enough to make a trench that could conceal a standing man. In these areas, the trenches were built up from ground level with sandbags filled with earth dug right on the spot. Sandbag parapets could be as high as eight to ten feet and sometimes as thick as eight feet to withstand machine-gun fire and shell bursts. The parados, also constructed of sandbags, had to be high enough to protect men in the trench from shells exploding behind them. This type of trench was known as a command trench, or box trench. It too was divided by traverses and included a fire step.

German trenches followed a similar pattern. Since the Germans had chosen higher ground for their trenches, they had less need for command trenches. The Germans had the luxury of choice: since they were fighting on enemy soil, they were willing to fall back a few hundred yards to build their trenches on a hill or a position that offered natural defenses. The British and French were under orders not to give up an inch of ground, which often resulted in their holding inferior positions for practically the duration of the war.

The French did not use traverses in building their trenches. Instead they dug the trench in a zigzag line to avoid enemy enfilading fire.

Between the opposing trenches lay "no-man's land." The width of this barren strip varied from sector to sector. The average was 250 yards, although it might be as much as 500 yards or as little as 10. In some areas, opposing sentries could cross bayonets, though this was not typical. The trenches were always close enough for each side to see the other.

In the beginning, there was only one trench line. As the war went on, additional trench lines were built to the rear of the front line. A typical trench defense would have three parallel lines. In front was the fire trench, the first line of defense against an enemy attack. Several hundred yards to the rear was a support trench where reinforcements would hold the line in case of an attack breaking through the front line. Cooking, first-aid stations, and other support services for the front-line trenches were often located here.

Farther to the rear were the reserve trenches where men assembled before being sent to the front lines. Billets were also located here for men to stay in when they were on relief from front-line duty.

The various trench lines were connected by communication trenches. These were narrower than the front-line trenches and generally followed a zigzag pattern to avoid enfilading fire. They ran for several miles to the relative safety of rear areas.

Directional signs popped up all over the trench walls, necessary since there were no landmarks to keep men from getting lost in the ever-growing maze. The men gave the trenches names taken from places back home. Regent Street and Strand were favorites with the British soldiers; a French trench might have a makeshift sign identifying it as the Rue de Rivoli or the Champs Elysées.

Troops serving in the front line were usually relieved within two to five days, although in battles they could serve there for weeks. Some provision had to be made for the men to sleep. Dugouts, rooms hollowed out beneath and behind the trench lines, were constructed for shelter, sleep, and storage. Larger dugouts in the rear trenches served as command posts and medical stations.

The dugouts varied greatly in comfort and size. They could

be little more than a "funk hole," or hollowed-out place where a soldier could catch a nap without being stepped on. Or they could be large and relatively comfortable rooms. Ernst Junger, a German soldier, described his dugout:

> I was master of an underground dwelling approached by forty steps hewn in the solid chalk . . . In one wall I had a bed . . . At its head hung an electric light . . . The whole was shut off from the outer world by a dark-red curtain with rod and rings.

Strongpoints of concrete or earthworks protected by barbed wire gave protection to machine guns, snipers, and trench mortars. Machine guns were spaced along the front so that the arc formed by the fire of one gun would intersect with the arc of the next gun along the line. This way, no-man's land and the entire front line of the enemy could be held under constant fire.

Heavy artillery was located two miles behind the front lines to keep it from capture. Nevertheless, the artillery had a range great enough to reach any point in the opposing trench system. Men in any part of the intricate network were always in danger from a surprise artillery attack.

The work of building trenches never really stopped. Artillery barrages, heavy rains, and grenades destroyed trenches and they had to be rebuilt. As the number of men used in attacks grew larger, more support trenches had to be built to accommodate them, and more communication trenches dug to allow them to move forward. The 475-mile front eventually encompassed many thousands of miles of trenches of all types.

The continual work of digging trenches involved a tremendous amount of work, all of which was done by the troops. All along the front, men who had come expecting to fight for their country found themselves armed with shovels, advancing not toward the enemy, but downward into the earth. The British army alone issued more than 10.5 million spades during the war. "I enlisted to save France," an English soldier complained, "not to shovel it into sacks."

Men reached the front lines aflame with wartime propaganda and ideals. They found a less glamorous war of digging, filling sandbags, laying down boards on the trench floor, rolling out barbed wire, and carrying all these materials through the miles of communication trenches. A sniper's bullet or artillery attack might strike them down before they ever saw an enemy soldier. For them the war was most of all the digging. The digging never ended.

The trench lines established in 1914 were to shift no more than eleven miles until the last year of the war. But the defensive strength of the trench positions enabled the commanders to pull some of their troops out of the line to build a reserve to go on the offensive elsewhere. There were two options: to break through the line or go around it. The year 1915 would see both these options tried, without success.

Germany could regard the first months of the war as a qualified success. Although stopped at the Marne from a decisive victory, the Germans controlled most of Belgium and part of northeast France. In the east, the Germans had won impressive victories over the Russians under Generals Paul von Hindenburg and Erich Ludendorff, the hero of Liège. But the Schlieffen Plan had failed—Germany had knocked neither Russia nor France out of the war, and were faced with the problem of conducting a two-front war.

Germany's allies gave certain advantages and disadvantages. United geographically to its major allies—Austria-Hungary, Turkey, and Bulgaria (which entered in 1915)—Germany could move troops and supplies by train between the eastern and western fronts. Unfortunately, Austria-Hungary was shaky politically and militarily. One German officer expressed his blunt opinion of Germany's principal ally: "We are chained to a corpse."

STRATEGY AND THE GENERALS

Falkenhayn wanted to concentrate his forces on the western front in 1915 to try for a breakthrough. He was overruled by the kaiser, who wanted to force Russia out of the war by capitalizing on the success of Hindenburg and Ludendorff. Afterwards, Germany could concentrate all its forces against France. The Germans would stay on the defensive in the west during 1915. There they would strengthen their defensive fortifications to repel attacks.

Britain and France on the Allied side were faced with different options. Although there was no unified Allied command, the French tended to decide major strategy since they were then making the greater contribution of troops. The British went along as a junior partner mounting supplementary attacks, although they planned their own campaigns.

Russia was cut off by land from Britain and France and suffered from lack of supplies and disorganization. It depended on its own resources and whatever supplies could be brought through by the British navy. Nonetheless, the vast manpower and land mass of Russia served to keep Germany from a final victory.

Among the advantages of the western allies were their vast empires. The French were able to employ troops from North Africa and Asia. The British Empire sent Indian, Canadian, Australian, and New Zealand soldiers. From the Battle of the Somme in 1916 to the end of the war, these troops would play a disproportionately large part in the Allied war effort.

Another Allied advantage was the superiority of the British navy. It established a blockade that the Germans could not break. As a result, Germany suffered from a shortage of war matériel and food. German resistance was gradually worn down by the continuing effectiveness of the blockade.

Some leaders on the Allied side, particularly in Britain,

wanted to solve the problem of the trench deadlock by attacking Austria-Hungary or Turkey in the south of Europe. Other leaders opposed these plans, insisting that victory must be won by liberating France and Belgium. Those who pressed for the opening of a second front were called "easterners"; the others were known as "westerners."

In 1915, the easterners had two chances. The British landed troops at Gallipoli near Constantinople, the capital of the Turkish Empire. But the British commanders didn't exploit their initial success. By January, 1916, the Allied positions were abandoned. Another "easterner" foray in 1915 was the landing of Allied troops in Salonika, Greece. Their mission was to aid the Serbians and eventually drive through Austria-Hungary to attack Germany. Unfortunately, troops from the Central Powers were able to keep the Allies bottled up in Salonika until the very end of the war.

The westerner position usually prevailed among Allied planners. For the French, their first goal was to drive the Germans from their soil. Despite the heavy casualties of 1914, French generals still clung to the possibilities of the offensive. Joffre was optimistic that in 1915 the French would break out of the stalemate. He planned a joint French-British attack on the German line around the Noyon salient, named for the town near its farthest extension.

The Noyon salient was the middle part of the gigantic "S" that the trench lines formed. Joffre planned to "pinch" the salient by attacking in the north in Artois and to the south in the Champagne region. The British were to launch supporting attacks in the north. Joffre's attacks began December 20, 1914. In Artois the attacks were rebuffed at once. In the Champagne region, a few German trenches were captured in the early fighting. But even after a month of assaults, with the French

French soldiers, with bayonets ready, charge through German barbed wire. If the wire had not been cut beforehand, which was frequently the case, attackers had to stop and cut their way through. LIBRARY OF CONGRESS

outnumbering the Germans four to one, the French advance was only a little more than a mile. In January, Joffre called off the attacks.

This early campaign illustrated the futile pattern of battle that would hold true through most of the war. Artillery bombardments and heavy concentrations of troops could usually break the first trench line. But strong secondary defenses kept the attackers from making a breakthrough that could be followed up and expanded.

Joffre did not see this pattern. He saw only the bright spot of the initial breakthrough in Champagne. He attributed the slowing of the attack to insufficient amounts of matériel and numbers of men. The Allies were steadily increasing their production of shells and weapons. In the fall, Joffre would be able to attack in force. Until then he planned to continue with small-scale attacks to "nibble away" at the German line.

On February 16, 1915, the French began a smaller offensive in the Champagne area. After a long bombardment the French went over the top. The attack had only limited success, but Joffre kept it going through March 30. The results were 240,000 casualties for the French and about 100,000 for the Germans. Once more the German positions had held.

Joffre was still not discouraged. The Allies were now building up their war matériel for a major assault in September. Once again, the Champagne region was chosen for an attack. The artillery bombardment would be greater than ever before, augmented by heavy guns that had been removed from the forts around Verdun.

But in the meantime the Germans had made advances in their defensive tactics. They planned a defense in depth. A second line of trenches would contain the greater part of the troops. There, only the heavy artillery could reach them.

With great *élan*, the French attacked, singing the "Marseillaise," their national anthem. In the first few hours they took the lightly defended first line of trenches. It took till the end of September to breach the second line, but the French could advance no further because by then German reserves had come up to close the gap in the line. The offensive was called off on October 8. The French proudly announced they had taken 25,000 prisoners, but failed to mention their casualties of 100,000 wounded and dead.

Coordinated with this attack was an offensive in the north under French General Ferdinand Foch. The French objective here was Vimy Ridge. Although French soldiers fought their way to the top in some places, they could never consolidate their positions. They suffered twice the casualties of the Germans.

Tied to the French offensives was a British attack at the town of Loos. On September 25, after a bombardment that included the use of gas shells, the British took Loos. Through Sir John French's inept handling of the reserves, however, the attack was stymied there. Now the British had only succeeded in opening a vulnerable salient that would be difficult to defend. General French was soon replaced by General Sir Douglas Haig.

The Allied generals looking at the sorry record of 1915 were still convinced that if only more matériel and manpower were used the breakthrough would occur. In each case, initial breakthroughs had been made, only to peter out when German reserves arrived. The generals' logic was compelling: more will do it.

But the emphasis on great masses of men and matériel sacrificed the advantages of surprise. And two attacks in 1915 clearly showed to the generals the power of a surprise attack.

French soldiers making their way into a German trench. The soldier
on the right is looking for hidden defenders in a German dugout. LI-
BRARY OF CONGRESS

University School
Media Center

A German assault team launches an attack. LIBRARY OF CONGRESS

One was the Battle of Neuve-Chapelle. This was the British contribution to Joffre's "nibbling away" attacks in the spring Champagne offensive. Neuve-Chapelle was the first time the British attacked against a fully developed German trench system.

The British had made careful preparations. Aerial reconnaissance had given them a complete outline of the German trenches. On March 10, the attack took place on a narrow front after an initial artillery bombardment of only thirty-five minutes. The British took the first line of trenches easily. Unprepared for this quick success, they could not bring their reserves up quickly enough to exploit it.

The generals drew some right and some wrong conclusions from Neuve-Chapelle. They realized correctly that the front had to be wider to enable more reserves to move quickly through the gap in the lines.

But the generals missed the significance of the initial breakthrough. They failed to see that the brief but intense artillery barrage had kept the Germans from making preparations for the attack. They felt that a heavier and longer bombardment would ensure success.

Another battle where the importance of surprise was overlooked was the Battle of Festubert in May, 1915. Short of shells, the British were unable to mount an effective artillery barrage. Nevertheless, the central force of attackers did break through although the flanking troops did not. The reason for the success was the fact that the battle was launched at night, at 12:30 A.M. The Germans were caught unawares by the unusual night attack.

Again the crucial factor of surprise was overlooked. The British were not to use night attacks again until more than a year later at the long Battle of the Somme.

The generals were not able to see that larger attacks caused the opposing side to build up its defenses. Thus a British attack on Aubers Ridge in May attempted to duplicate the success of the early stages at Neuve-Chapelle. At Aubers the British assembled more troops and used a heavier bombardment, but they were firmly repulsed, with no breakthrough. The reason was that in the two months since Neuve-Chapelle, the Germans had constructed stronger fortifications. The stronger defenses repulsed a stronger attack.

This problem was really never solved in the war. Artillery bombardments and offensives grew larger and larger as the generals doggedly clung to the idea that if only a large enough attack could be mounted, it would achieve breakthrough. But mass force only spelled mass slaughter, not victory.

Inadequate mechanization of the armies in the field was one key reason why defensive forces could close the line after an initial penetration by superior forces. Behind the lines, railroads brought troops to the battlefield. Once there, however, they had to advance on foot. There was little use of motorized transport at the front. The mud and craters caused by the huge artillery bombardment made advancing across no-man's land and through the trench system a slow process. Attackers thus were slow to exploit a breakthrough, while the enemy was moving reinforcements by train to plug the hole in the line.

The total casualty figures for the Allies on the western front during 1915 were about 1.5 million men—in return for ridiculously small gains in territory. As the figures and the extent of the disaster became known, the troops took a scornful attitude toward the generals. Staff officers—those who took part in the command decisions—were identified by insignia on their uniforms. In the British army, they wore red tabs, which came to be known in the front lines as "badges of shame."

A German military dog, carrying messages from the front lines, jumps over a support trench. The message roll can be seen around his neck. All the armies used dogs and pigeons to carry messages as they were more dependable than more modern methods. Telephone and telegraph wires were too often broken by the continual artillery barrages.
NATIONAL ARCHIVES

Adding to the troops' contempt was the fact that the staff officers maintained headquarters far to the rear of the battlefield, sometimes in French châteaus whose luxury contrasted with the filth of the trenches. Siegfried Sassoon, a British soldier, recorded the comment of a soldier on passing "the general's white château" that the officers must suffer terribly from insomnia with so many guns firing only fifteen miles away.

The generals were widely believed to be incompetent as well. Guy Empey, an American who served with the British early in the war, wrote about capturing a German soldier, who told him

> German snipers get paid rewards for killing the English. . . . For killing or wounding an English private, the sniper gets one mark. For killing or wounding an English officer he gets five marks, but if he kills a Red Cap or English general, the sniper gets 21 days tied to the wheel of a limber [cart] as punishment for his carelessness. . . . If all the English generals were killed, there would be no one left to make costly mistakes.

The troops did respect and like the junior officers, "line" officers, who shared the dangers of the trenches and led the attacks. These officers suffered higher casualties than any other group, including enlisted men.

Senior officers were rarely seen at the front. They avoided the sight of horribly wounded men, feeling it might affect their judgment in ordering the brutal attacks. General Haig "felt that it was his duty to refrain from visiting the casualty clearing stations because these visits made him physically ill." And Joffre, after pinning a medal on a blinded soldier, said, "I mustn't be shown any more such spectacles . . . I would no longer have the courage to give the order to attack."

The inability of the generals to form an effective strategy stemmed in part from their background and training. Many of the officers of all three armies came from aristocratic backgrounds and had experience in the cavalry, which the trenches had rendered obsolete. Their personal experience with the technology which produced the truly powerful weapons of the war was slight. The command staffs included no scientific advisers for evaluating new weapons and suggesting uses for them. Modern armies had become so large that the command staffs could no longer effectively control them. Often the generals did not know the situation on the battlefield until it was too late. The wireless radio was still in its infancy; military communications still largely depended on runners and dogs and carrier pigeons. Nor would a general at the battlefield have been any more effective: he could not have seen the scope of the vast battle nor given orders to his forces.

The generals went on attacking in the old way. Their optimism led them to believe they were damaging the enemy more than they really were. The strategy of attrition—wearing down the enemy through losses of men and matériel—came to be the excuse for the horrible casualty figures. Attrition was Haig's justification for some of his biggest failures. "Bleed the enemy white" was Falkenhayn's strategy at Verdun. But the offensive side lost as much or more than those on the defensive, and given the equality of forces between the two sides, attrition was a self-defeating strategy.

One of two things was necessary to break the deadlock: new tactics that would make a breakthrough possible, or new weapons that would finally make the offensive stronger than the defensive. The Germans would find the tactics, and the Allies the weapon.

The mass bloodshed of World War I would not have been possible without the advances in weaponry that had taken place in the last half of the nineteenth century. And throughout the war the search continued for the ultimate weapon that would tip the balance in the trench stalemate to one side or the other.

Artillery was used in the war on a scale never before seen. Four developments in artillery made it more effective than ever before. These were breech loading, smokeless powder, quick-firing mechanisms, and rifled barrels.

Breech loading enabled crews to work artillery weapons behind armored shields; no longer did they have to expose themselves by going to the front of the cannon to load. Likewise, smokeless powder, which now permitted the gunners to continue to see their targets throughout a mass artillery attack; the black powder used previously created so much smoke that the gunners were effectively firing blind after a few minutes. Smokeless powder also left less of a residue so that guns could be fired longer without extensive cleaning.

In 1897, the French developed a secret gun—the "75." (Sizes of guns are measured by the diameter of the bore, or barrel; this was a 75-millimeter gun, or about 3 inches.) The 75 combined breech loading with a hydraulic-and-spring action that absorbed the recoil of the gun. The result was the first quick-firing (QF) artillery weapon that did not have to be rolled back

THE WEAPONS 4

into place for every shot. Skilled crews could fire it as quickly as twenty times a minute. The 75 didn't remain a secret long, and other nations developed their own QF artillery.

Rifled barrels and shells were the fourth major development in artillery before the war. As late as the American Civil War, cannon had still fired metal balls. Rifled artillery shells had grooves cut into their sides that imparted a spin to the new, bullet-shaped shells. The spin increased the range and accuracy of shellfire in the same way that a spiral gives accuracy and distance to a thrown football.

Field guns such as the 75 were designed for fighting in open fields, where swift movement was a part of the battle. In such a situation, the lightness of the gun was an asset, even though it limited the size of the shells that could be used.

Since swift-moving attacks were all but impossible in trench fighting, artillery planners soon began to mount huge artillery pieces on railroad cars and bring them to the front. These behemoths had previously been fired only from ships, in naval attacks. Now it was possible to fling a shell weighing a ton or more several miles (one could fire up to eighty miles) on targets that could not even be seen by the gunners.

The use of airplanes and Zeppelins (called "sausages" by the men in the trenches) contributed to the accuracy of these huge new guns. Spotters from airplanes could see precisely how far away enemy targets were and where the shells were falling.

With air surveillance came the need for camouflage. At first foliage and debris were used to hide emplacements. As time went on, special support units were organized to create camouflage. Artists were assigned to the units to paint large canvases that were placed between the branches of trees.

The old-time field gun had another disadvantage besides size that made it ineffective in trench warfare. It was designed to fire on a relatively flat trajectory toward an unprotected mass of men or a walled building. In the trenches, the shells now slammed into reinforced trench parapets or went flying over the trenches altogether, sparing the soldiers hiding within.

Howitzers and mortars proved more effective in this kind of fighting. These had steeper trajectories of fire. Their shells dropped down from above into the trenches and even into the dugouts beneath. Mortars and howitzers were often as big as or bigger than the field guns.

The Germans had a series of mortars called *Minnenwerfers* (or "Minnies") that ranged in size from three to seven inches. The Minnies could be used close to the front lines and were very accurate. They proved so effective that the British soldiers devised their own makeshift mortars out of steel pipes and fired scrap metal from them. Later, British industry developed the Stokes mortar, which had the mobility and accuracy of the lighter German *Minnenwerfers*.

Different types of shells were developed for different purposes. Shrapnel shells contained a charge of powder and several hundred metal projectiles. The charge went off a certain number of seconds after the shell had been fired, showering the enemy trenches with deadly shrapnel. There were several kinds of exploding shells: some exploded before they hit, some on impact, and some were delayed-action shells that buried themselves in the ground before exploding. There were also shells containing various types of poison gases.

The men in the trenches could distinguish between different types of shells by the sounds they made as they approached. British soldiers called the large 210-millimeter German shells "Jack Johnsons." These fell with a high-pitched whistle and exploded with a black cloud of smoke. (Jack Johnson was the black American heavyweight champion of the day.) A lighter

A Krupp 340 mm. naval gun firing. Such guns, intended for use on battleships, were mounted on railway cars and sent to add firepower to the immense artillery duels on the western front. NATIONAL ARCHIVES

shell that made a very brief buzzing sound less than a second before it arrived was called the "whizz bang." Shrapnel shells, because of the "singing" of the hundreds of pieces of metal that flew through the air after they exploded, were known as "musical instruments."

The shells were not always reliable. Some exploded in the guns, killing their crews. This type of accident occurred so frequently with a certain type of howitzer shell that howitzer crews began calling themselves "suicide clubs."

Other crews fired numerous "shorts"—shells that fell short of their target and landed on their own trenches. One German unit, the 49th Field Artillery Regiment, was so notorious for its shorts that the men in the trenches called it the 48½th.

Although the horror of trench fighting was intensified by the near-constant artillery barrages, the trench stalemate was caused by the power of the machine gun. The machine gun came to represent the use of technology applied to weaponry. It was a *machine,* giving power to a single man far beyond his ordinary ability as an individual.

The feelings of a soldier facing masses of machine guns was expressed by Henri Barbusse, describing a French platoon waiting to attack: "Each one knows that he is going to take his head, his chest, his belly, his whole body, and all naked, up to the rifles pointed forward, to the shells, to the bombs piled and ready, and above all to the methodical and almost infallible machine guns."

The Germans were first to realize the importance of the machine gun. Between 1905 and 1908, each infantry regiment in the German army was equipped with rapid-firing Maxims, an early type of machine gun. At the beginning of the war, the German army had more than forty-five hundred machine guns, compared with twenty-five hundred for France and fewer than five hundred in the British army. The attitude of the British high command was stated by General Douglas Haig at the beginning of the war: "The machine gun is a much overrated weapon and two per battalion are more than sufficient." By the end of the war, the British had more than forty machine guns per battalion.

One of the most feared of the new weapons was gas, though it actually accounted for far fewer casualties than either machine guns or artillery. The first effective use of gas on the western front was by the Germans at the Second Battle of Ypres on April 22, 1915. The Germans carried over five thousand large cylinders of chlorine gas to their front-line trenches on a three-and-a-half-mile front. They waited for the wind to begin blowing east to west and in the late afternoon of the twenty-second, they opened the valves on the cylinders.

Neither side was prepared for the effect of the gas. French colonial troops from Algeria manned the Allied trenches in that area. They saw a strange green cloud drifting toward them and when it reached their lines, they panicked. The effect of chlorine gas is intense pain in the nose and throat, followed by inability to breathe. Victims lay choking to death where the gas passed by. Some of the soldiers were able to run out of the way of the gas cloud and report the news to headquarters.

Headquarters had already received word from captured German prisoners that a gas attack was planned, but when it failed to take place on the date given (because the wind was wrong), the Allied command dismissed the report as a hoax. As a result, there were no reinforcements to plug the five-mile-wide gap that now stood in the Allied lines.

But the German command was equally unprepared for its success. They didn't realize that the front was open, nor were there enough German reinforcements to take advantage of the

A German soldier hurling one of the "potato masher" grenades. A strong thrower could throw one of these 40 or 50 yards with some accuracy. LIBRARY OF CONGRESS

gap. Also, German troops were reluctant to advance into the gassed area because traces of the gas still lingered.

Canadian soldiers were moved up to fill the gap in the Allied line. They used hastily improvised gas masks made of cotton bandages soaked in water, bicarbonate of soda, or urine.

The British and French began to develop their own gas weapons after Ypres. (In a concession to public opinion, the British military never referred to "gas"; it was always called "the accessory.") Both Allies and Germans soon developed more efficient gas masks, which were worn by men, horses, and even army dogs. Most masks were hot, stuffy, and hard to see out of. Gas attacks thus limited a soldier's effectiveness, even though he was protected from harm.

Both sides developed new gases. Among the most important were phosgene, which acted like chlorine but was ten times as powerful, and mustard gas, which burned the skin, eyes, and tissues of the nose and throat. New protective masks and clothing were developed for each new gas.

They were not always effective. A nurse wrote: "I wish those people who write so glibly about this being a holy war . . . could see the poor things . . . with blind eyes . . . all sticky and stuck together, and always fighting for breath, with voices a mere whisper, saying that their throats are closing and they know they will choke."

Gas attacks launched from containers could backfire if the wind suddenly shifted, blowing the gas back on the troops that had released it. To solve this problem, the French discovered a way to fill artillery shells with gas. This added a new choice to the arsenal of the artillery officer. Shells filled with smoke were also used as concealment for attacking forces.

When an enemy raid or attack breached the opposing lines, the hand-to-hand fighting that followed required its own special weapons. Some of these reduced warfare to the most basic level. The equipment in one British unit included a "persuader," or club about two feet long. The thick end was studded with steel spikes and through the center of the club ran a lead bar to give it weight and balance. The same unit had several "knuckle knives," which were daggers about eight inches long with heavy steel guards over the grip. "One punch in the face generally shatters a man's jaw and you can get him with the knife as he goes down," wrote one soldier.

Another weapon for close trench fighting was the hand grenade. Lobbing these into the enemy trenches preparatory to entering the trench from no-man's land was one way of ensuring a polite welcome. They were also used for clearing and consolidating trenches.

Many kinds of grenades were manufactured during the war, some almost as dangerous to the user as to the intended victim. A kind used early by the British was designed to explode when it landed on its head. In the close quarters of the trenches, a grenadier drawing back to throw one of these could strike the back wall of the trench with it. The number of duds and defective grenades that exploded prematurely gave grenadiers membership rights in the growing "suicide club."

Early in the war, the troops concocted their own makeshift grenades out of jam containers, gunpowder, and whatever shrapnel could be found to add to the mix. A fuse was placed on the can, lighted like a match against a wooden slat strapped to the arm, and thrown over the top.

The best official British grenade design was introduced in 1915. Known as the Mills bomb, it was about the size and shape of a large lemon, but with a cast-iron exterior that was divided into forty-eight square sections that caused the men to nickname it "the pineapple." The sectioning of the case was de-

British soldiers who were victims of a gas attack. Most are blinded, and hold onto the shoulder of the man ahead as they wait their turn at a treatment station. IMPERIAL WAR MUSEUM

Two British machine gunners found dead at their posts by a German cameraman. The wall of the heavily reinforced pillbox in which machine guns were often placed can be seen. When enemy troops overran the trench lines, however, machine gunners were vulnerable to attack from the rear. LIBRARY OF CONGRESS

signed to cause the bomb to shatter into many lethal fragments when it exploded.

The best-known German grenade was called from its shape the "potato masher." A wooden handle attached to a canister of explosives made it possible for German soldiers to throw the potato masher as far as sixty yards. The British later introduced a similar model, which was dubbed the "hairbrush."

In October, 1914, the Germans introduced the *Flammenwerfer,* or flamethrower, which spewed forth flaming gasoline, against French troops. Later the British and French developed their own models. Though it was frightening, the flamethrower was not particularly effective as a trench weapon. The British models weighed up to two tons and required three hundred separate trips to bring the pieces for one model to the front lines. They were useful only for clearing a small section of line, and their range was only about ninety yards. They were not portable enough to be moved forward in attacks.

Another development, called the Livens projector, proved more effective in the trenches. The projector was a device similar to a small mortar. Using empty oil drums sunk in the ground as gun barrels, the British soldiers loaded them with an explosive charge and fired a variety of objects toward German trenches. Small containers of gasoline, shrapnel, or gas could all be launched from Livens projectors. Banks of the projectors could cover an opposing line in a wall of flame or cloud of gas.

The tank, first developed in World War I, was the weapon that could have broken the trench stalemate. Unfortunately, it was never used to its full effectiveness till the end of the war.

A British colonel named Sir Ernest Swinton had seen American caterpillar-track vehicles used to transport artillery. He saw the possibility of attaching these caterpillar tracks to armored and armed vehicles for offensive purposes. Winston

Churchill, first lord of the admiralty, championed Swinton's idea. He persuaded the British government to authorize tests. To ensure secrecy, the chassis and the hull of the new vehicle were manufactured in different places. When the hull was being made, workers were told it was a water tank for desert fighting, and the name stuck.

Testing proved the tank could roll over barbed wire and trenches as wide as ten feet. Its firepower consisted of two Lewis machine guns and two small-bore artillery guns. Even so, the military leaders were doubtful about its effectiveness. They requested only forty vehicles. Lord Kitchener, minister of war, called the tank "a pretty, mechanical toy . . . The war will never be won by such machines." Later, at Churchill's urging, the order was increased to 150 tanks.

Swinton set to work training men to operate the tanks. It was not an enviable assignment. The model Mark IV, which was used at the Battle of Cambrai in 1917, had a crew of eight. Since the noise of the engine made shouted orders impossible, the commander of the crew banged on the metal hull with a hammer, using a preset code. Each tread of the tank had its own operator, or gearsman. If the commander wanted to turn left, the right-side gearsman had to operate his tread, while the gearsman on the left would disengage his tread. The tank could go only six miles an hour. After thirty minutes of use, the temperature inside the tank rose to over 100 degrees. There was no room for the crew to stand or move around. The engine was mounted inside and its fumes and noise added to the suffering of the crew.

Churchill and Swinton urged that a large force of tanks be used for a major try at a breakthrough. But General Haig decided to use the few tanks he had at the Battle of the Somme.

A *flammenwerfer* spraying an attacking British tank on the Somme front. The Germans allowed the tank to creep close to make escape impossible. The tank crew was burned to death, trapped inside when their gasoline tank exploded. NATIONAL ARCHIVES

Instead of massing them together, he scattered the tanks throughout his front line.

Though few in number, the tanks at the Somme had a spectacular effect. German troops turned and ran from what a German journalist described as "mysterious monsters ... slowly hobbling, rolling, and rocking ... Nothing impeded them. A supernatural force seemed to impel them forward. Someone in the trenches said, 'The devil is coming,' and the word passed along the line."

German soldiers began to fling grenades at the tanks; some were effective. Other tanks suffered mechanical breakdowns. Despite their initial panic, the Germans soon regrouped before the British could make any substantial gains. German commanders were unimpressed. Their reaction was to build "tank traps"—ditches that would be too wide for tanks to pass over.

Germany failed to try to develop tanks of its own until too late in the war to make a difference. France, working independently, developed its own tanks. Theirs were designed to be lighter and faster than the British models, but were not used until the last year of the war.

After the Somme, Haig asked for 1,000 additional tanks. It was not until late in 1917, however, at the Battle of Cambrai, that tanks were used in a mass formation to make a major advance. Even after Cambrai, the British generals were still groping for a way to coordinate tanks effectively with infantry advances.

The lesson of the generals' use of weapons in World War I was that military thinking had not kept pace with technology. It would require another twenty years—the interval between the world wars—for commanders and military thinkers to develop effective ways of using the terrible weapons that grew out of World War I.

The most dreaded words of World War I were the order to go "over the top." The men in the trenches knew that these words, sending them over the trench wall to no-man's land, were a death sentence for many, if not most, of the first wave of infantry.

The night before an attack, the men tried to take their minds off what tomorrow might bring. Yet all the necessary preparations reminded them of awaiting death. Each man wrote a letter home, which was turned over to an officer to be mailed if the writer was killed. The letters informed loved ones that the writer was dead. Each man also wrote a last will and testament in the official booklet that recorded army pay due him.

Usually the men waited in dugouts that were safe from enemy shells. Both sides were by now engaged in an all-out artillery barrage that could go on for hours, even days. A German soldier described the scene as he waited in a reserve trench for the order to attack.

> There we lay the whole day . . . crouching in the narrow trench on a thin layer of straw, in an overpowering din which never ceased all day or the greater part of the night—the whole ground trembling and shaking . . .

Attacks generally came at dawn. As the time drew near, the men shouldered their heavy packs, weighing as much as sixty

OVER THE TOP  5

Canadian troops going "over the top." The Canadians, along with the
Australian and New Zealand troops were among the most effective
fighters in the war. The heavy packs which encumbered the soldiers
as they ran toward enemy lines can be seen in this picture. NATIONAL
ARCHIVES

pounds. If gas was being used by either side, gas masks were donned, making it harder to see and breathe. Scaling ladders were placed against the parapet if it was a high one. Bayonets were fixed on the ends of rifles. Sometimes a smoke screen was released from the front-line trenches.

No one could look over the top at no-man's land, but each man knew that it would be covered with craters made by the falling shells, yards and yards of barbed wire, and raked with continual machine-gun fire. By nightfall the craters and the wire would be full of the bodies of fallen and dead.

The word passed down the line: "ten minutes to go." *Ten minutes to live!* one soldier recalled thinking. Those in their first battle were worried they might not be able to force themselves to go over the top. "There you have a brave young chap," wrote a French officer. "It was his first 'show.' He was sweating with fear, shaking with fear. . . . He gripped his rifle, he threw himself forward . . . and he went because he had to go. He was afraid of nothing so much as showing his fear."

Patrick MacGill, a member of a British medical unit, had another explanation for the men's ability to throw themselves toward enemy fire:

> All men have some restraining influence to help them
> in hours of trial, some principle or some illusion.
> Duty, patriotism, vanity, and dreams come to the help
> of men in the trenches, all illusions probably,
> ephemeral and fleeting; but for a man who is as
> ephemeral and fleeting as his illusions are, he can lay
> his back against them and defy death and the terrors
> of the world.

The first men are ordered onto the ladders. "There is never any pushing or crowding to be first up these ladders," one soldier noted. Then comes the terrible moment of silence as the barrage stops. Officers blow their whistles to signal the attack. Sergeants push the first men upward with a cry of "Over the top with the best of luck!" Shouting in fear, rage, or defiance, the men throw themselves over the top.

For some, that was as far as they got.

Robert Graves, an English officer, wrote of a platoon that went over the top only to throw themselves to the ground immediately to avoid machine-gun fire. When the officer blew his whistle to signal advance again, no one moved. "You bloody cowards," he called, "are you leaving me to go on alone?" The platoon sergeant lifted himself on a shattered arm and said, "Not cowards, sir. Willing enough. But they're all f——ing dead."

Some advanced through the fire toward the enemy trench line. One man wrote: "I had been worried by the thought: 'Suppose one should lose one's head and get other men cut up! Suppose one's legs should take fright and refuse to move!' Now I knew it was all right. I shouldn't be frightened and I shouldn't lose my head."

Barbed wire blocking the way was supposed to be cut by patrols the night before the attack. Often it wasn't, and attackers had to cut the wire by hand while all around them men were falling to the enemy machine guns. Behind them, more men were swarming over the sides of the trenches, and would keep coming.

The smoke and noise caused men to lose their way. They might run along the barbed wire, looking for a place to get through, or become totally confused and run toward their own trenches, firing blindly. The wounded who could crawl were trying to make it back to their own lines, where they were only a hindrance to be carried away to make room for the new men coming up through the trench system. Out in no-man's land, the medical corpsman MacGill saw "men and bits of men lying all over the place. A leg, an arm, then again a leg, cut off at the hip." MacGill stopped to bandage a man.

> A big high-explosive shell flew over our heads and dropped fifty yards away in a little hollow where seven or eight figures in khaki lay prostrate, faces to the ground. The shell burst and the wounded and dead rose slowly into the air to a height of six or seven yards and dropped slowly again, looking for all the world like puppets worked by wires.

Somehow, men made it through to the opposing trench line. If a man was lucky, he found a trench that had been hit by a shell and was occupied now only by corpses. The attackers flung grenades into occupied trenches. Men followed the grenade explosions, flailing about with bayonets, clubs, or knives.

Guy Empey described one instance of hand-to-hand combat in a trench attack. "A huge Prussian" was fighting "three little Tommies" (British soldiers). The bayonet from the German's rifle was gone, and he was clutching the barrel in both hands and swinging the butt around his head. "The Tommy nearest me," wrote Empey,

> received the butt of the German's rifle in a smashing blow below the right temple. It smashed his head like an eggshell. He pitched forward on his side and a convulsive shudder ran through his body. Meanwhile, the other Tommy had gained the rear of the Prussian. Suddenly about four inches of bayonet protruded from the throat of the Prussian soldier, who staggered forward and fell. I will never forget the look of blank astonishment that came over his face.

Fatigue shows on these German machine gunners, covered with mud and resting on a narrow ledge to keep out of the knee deep water in the trench behind them. LIBRARY OF CONGRESS

After a section of trench had been taken, the men tried to extend their position. They flung grenades over the next traverse, to avoid meeting a knife-wielding enemy on the other side. The attackers worked their way down the trench from fire bay to fire bay. When a group of men had taken as many fire bays as they could defend, they would "consolidate" the trench. This meant blocking it off at both ends to avoid counterattacks from another part of the trench.

Once a line of enemy trench was consolidated, a new parapet facing the next line had to be built. There was also the dangerous work of clearing the dugouts underneath, where enemy stragglers or wounded might be waiting with grenade or rifle.

Sometimes a small group of men would consolidate a short section of trench only to find that the rest of their attack force had been driven back. Enemy counterattacks would either obliterate them or force them back into no-man's land, where they would have to fight their way back to their home trenches.

During and after a battle, one of the most dangerous jobs was that of the stretcher bearers. It took four to six men to carry one wounded man back through no-man's land and down through the communication trenches to first-aid stations. If a man was wounded badly, he might be sent back to the support trench, where ambulances could take him to a field hospital. The only way to transport a man through the trench system was by stretcher. All the while, the trench system was under bombardment and clogged with soldiers moving the other way toward the fire trench.

In muddy, shell-blasted areas like Ypres and the Somme, stretcher bearers could take an hour just to bring one man to the first-aid station. Many of the wounded bled to death where they fell. The unburied dead, after a day or two in the sun, began to stink and were a health hazard. Usually, the two sides would have a truce after a battle to allow removal of bodies.

Sometimes the artillery fire along a line of battle continued for days, making rescue of the wounded or removal of the dead impossible. "Do not ask about the fate of the wounded!" a German soldier wrote home. "Anybody who was incapable of walking to the doctor had to die a miserable death . . . the combatants stormed regardlessly to and fro over them . . . A dog, dying in the poorest hovel at home, is enviable by comparison."

Robert Graves recalled a wounded officer who lay groaning in no-man's land. Several men tried to rescue him, only to be hit themselves. The man sent word back that he was dying, and that no more rescue attempts were to be made. "He sent his apologies to the company for making such a noise." Graves went out at dusk, and found the man "hit in 17 places. I found that he had forced his knuckles into his mouth to stop himself crying out and attracting any more men to their death."

Most of these frontal attacks through no-man's land gained little ground, though casualties were almost always heavy. One of the most wasteful of these frontal assaults was the Battle of the Somme, which took place from July to November, 1916.

The offensive at the Somme River was planned by the French, but the Battle of Verdun, which had started in February, 1916, and was still going on, shifted the burden to the British.

General Sir Douglas Haig, commander of the BEF, had had the cream of Britain's young men at his disposal. The "New Army" of volunteers who flocked to Kitchener's call for men now formed the bulk of the British army in France.

Many of them were organized in the so-called "Pals Battalions." In these, volunteers enlisted in groups to serve together throughout the war. Many villages in Britain saw almost their entire populations of military-age men enlist in the Pals battalions. Clubs, factories, offices, and schools also sent men to serve together. This was an effective way to recruit men because peer pressure was often sufficient to attract volunteers who otherwise might have been reluctant. Unfortunately, the officers of the "New Army" were new as well, and the men were very often inadequately trained before being sent to the front.

The Somme was to be Haig's first major campaign as commander in chief. Having criticized the commander he replaced, he was under pressure to do better. His objectives for the battle were to relieve pressure on the French at Verdun by inflicting losses on the Germans and to position the British for the "final victory" the following year.

Haig's plan called for the British Fourth Army, under General Sir Henry Rawlinson, to carry the main attack with twelve divisions in the initial thrust, keeping seven more in reserve. Behind Rawlinson's army was a reserve army of three infantry and three cavalry divisions commanded by General Sir Hubert Gough. Gough's cavalry was to attack after Rawlinson's men had broken the German line, to pursue and destroy retreating enemy units. The reserve infantry would occupy the front line of trenches on the German side while Rawlinson's main forces moved up to the support trenches.

To the right of Rawlinson's army was the French Sixth Army, consisting of five active and seven reserve divisions. Their task was to penetrate and hold the German positions in front of them, protecting the flank of the main force. On the left, the British Third Army was to mount diversionary attacks to draw the Germans away from the sector in front of Rawlinson.

Besides the men of the New Army, Haig had new weapons

and equipment at his disposal. The British had almost four hundred airplanes observing and mapping German trenches. The British constructed a scale model of the German trench system and used it for training. Detailed maps of the front were distributed to line commanders, complete with English names for each German trench, so each British unit could familiarize itself with its objective beforehand.

At the Somme steel helmets were issued to British troops for the first time. (Previously they had had leather ones.) A British model of the flamethrower was introduced, as were smoke bombs and gas-filled shells designed for use with the Stokes mortars.

Haig was confident. He promised Prime Minister David Lloyd George that if casualties were too great the battle would be called off.

On June 24, fifteen hundred British guns and two thousand French guns began a five-day-long barrage along an 18-mile front. Haig planned to make the barrage so devastating that the new British troops could walk across no-man's land shoulder to shoulder. The New Army having had insufficient training, it was thought wiser to send them across in the simplest possible formation. After such a heavy barrage, presumably there would be few German soldiers alive in the front-line trenches to offer resistance.

At the end of the fourth day of the barrage, it began to rain. The attack was held up for three more days, during which the barrage continued around the clock, using all available ammunition.

As the British troops came forward through the communication trenches, they saw their artillery crews, exhausted from the week-long, never-ending barrage, shirtless, dirty, and

British soldiers, having captured a section of German trench, erect a sign marking their victory. "Huns," actually barbarians of ancient Europe, were what the Allies unflatteringly called the Germans. The man in center and the man in the foreground have wrapped their rifles in rags to keep mud from clogging them. IMPERIAL WAR MUSEUM

As a German shell lands nearby, a British officer leads his men over the top to attack. The narrow trench shown here was typical of communication trenches. NATIONAL ARCHIVES

sweating from the heat of the guns. Some of the gunners were bleeding from the ears as a result of the perpetual din.

Each night in the final week, patrols went out to check the damage wrought by the barrage. Stokes mortars had been trained on the German barbed wire to cut it. Patrols found that most of the Stokes shells were duds that landed harmlessly in the midst of the wire. As one observer put it, they "riddled the ground like soccer balls." Headquarters disregarded this report, and ignored as well the heavy casualties suffered by the patrols, which indicated that there were still soldiers alive in the German front trenches.

On July 1, at 7:30 A.M., the order was given to go over the top. Silence fell as the shelling stopped. The German survivors in their reinforced dugouts deep underground grabbed their stacked weapons as they ran up the steps.

One of the Germans later wrote of the sight that awaited them: "We were very surprised to see them walking, we had never seen that before. . . . The officers went in front. I noticed one of them walking calmly, carrying a walking stick. When we started firing . . . they went down in their hundreds. You didn't have to aim. We just fired into them."

The long British lines wavered and crumpled. But the men regrouped and did the natural thing: they began running, seeking cover wherever they found it. Through some miracle of spirit, they continued to advance.

The attacking soldiers discovered that more than two-thirds of the barbed wire was left uncut, trapping them in no-man's land. Behind them, men were still streaming out of the trenches, while in front of them the German machine guns rattled on. Men tried to force their way through the wire, got caught, and were riddled with bullets. The weight of their bodies pulled the wire down, and their comrades followed, leaping over the pile of writhing wounded and dead.

A few of the British troops and the French troops on the right wing made it through to the first German trench line. There, they struggled with bayonets, clubs, knives, anything they could pick up in a fierce, primitive battle for survival. Those who captured trenches had to fight off counterattacks coming from the German second line where, alerted by the barrage, thousands of reserve troops had assembled in the week before the attack.

According to one estimate more than thirty thousand British troops were killed or wounded in the first hour of the fighting at the Somme. Because communications between the front and command headquarters miles behind the lines were so poor, no one at headquarters grasped what was happening. Men had been assigned to carry rolls of telephone wire through no-man's land with the troops to maintain communications, but they didn't get through.

Messages back and forth to the front-line troops had to be sent by runner. The runners were constantly exposed to enemy fire, and often never got through. The troops' contempt for the headquarters staff can be understood by looking at some of the messages that were sent.

A captain of volunteers recalled receiving a message in the middle of the battle. One man had been hit trying to deliver it. A second man brought it through. It read, "Please resubmit drawing of the foot of Pte. Warke, size of boot 13." "I was furious that such a stupid message should be sent at such a time and stamped it into the mud," said the captain.

Another staff officer sent this message during the first day's attack, to *many* of the front-line units:

Certain complaints have been received that no pork can be found in the [cans]. . . . Troops must not be misled by the name *pork* and beans, and expect to find a full ration of pork; as a matter of fact the pork is practically all absorbed by the beans.

Officers serving in the trenches with the men—line officers—earned their respect. A greater percentage of officers than men were casualties at the Somme. But men whose officers had been killed were left to wander aimlessly about the no-man's land, adding to the confusion and carnage, and making the attack a disorganized chaos.

The first day of the battle, the British army suffered the greatest losses it has ever suffered in one day: sixty thousand casualties. The attack was a dismal failure. Only Rawlinson's XIII Corps, to the right of the main attack, had succeeded in making any real gains. The corps had made use of a new kind of artillery barrage. Instead of the barrage stopping just before the troops went over the top, it continued as the troops advanced across no-man's land to the enemy trenches, keeping the enemy bottled up till the men arrived. This was called a "rolling" or "creeping" barrage because it could be coordinated to move with the troops from objective to objective across the enemy lines.

On the right flank, the French forces had done better than the British. The Germans had lightly defended that part of the front, expecting that Verdun had so weakened the French army that they could no longer mount a powerful attack. Also, the French had advanced in small, quickly moving groups, rather than long lines of walking men.

Amazingly, Haig ordered the attack to continue. Sometimes

A soldier wounded in an attack waits to be carried back to the rear lines for medical care. The other three soldiers are in what the British called "funk-holes," hastily dug shelters from exploding shell fire. NATIONAL ARCHIVES

the British made gains. On July 14, Rawlinson planned a surprise attack at night that punched out a salient four miles wide and a thousand yards deep, breaking through the Germans' second line. But the British command delayed nine hours before bringing up troops to exploit the break. By that time German reserves had arrived in force, closing the line again.

On September 15, Haig used tanks for the first time in the war to make a gap in the German lines that the cavalry galloped through—one of the last cavalry charges in the history of warfare. But the infantry and artillery could not keep up. German counterattacks caught the cavalry units without support and cut them to pieces.

The German commander in chief, Falkenhayn, ordered offensives to retake every yard of trench lost to the Allies. These attacks were as wasteful as Haig's strategy of attrition. Attack followed futile attack; as the summer rains came and the artillery continued, the ground became churned into an impassable bog. On November 13, the last attack took place. Snow stopped the generals at last from throwing more men over the top. There had been no breakthrough. In some places the Allied line had advanced seven miles; in other places, not at all.

For these gains, the British suffered 420,000 casualties; the French lost more than 200,000 men. No one knows the German losses with certainty. Some historians put it at 450,000 because of the wasteful attacks ordered by Falkenhayn.

Statistics do not tell the story adequately. For Britain, the best men of a whole generation perished at the Somme. The casualties Germany suffered brought home the possibility of defeat for the first time. The Germans' morale never completely recovered.

In personal terms, the loss is incomprehensible. Because of the British "pals" system of recruitment, some villages suffered devastating losses. "We were two years in the making and ten minutes in the destroying," one soldier recalled.

Martin Middleton, a historian of the battle, wrote of one town's loss:

> In Accrington (which had sent 700 men into action at the Somme) it was rumored that only seven men had survived from their Pals' attack! No one would confirm or deny the report and the townspeople surrounded the mayor's house in an angry mood.

The truth proved to be bad enough: 585 of Accrington's 700 were lost at the Somme.

After the battle, letters and packages for the dead continued to arrive at the trenches. It was agreed that the survivors should divide up the packages, most of which contained food. Middleton quotes the experience recalled by one of the survivors: "I chose two tins of sugar from a parcel. On opening them, there were two half-crowns in each tin—one from 'Mother' and one from 'Dad.' It all seemed so ghastly."

Rarely in the history of warfare have conditions for the regular fighting man been so terrible as they were in the trenches of World War I. One of the horrors was that warfare never really ceased, and as years passed, the men of both sides despaired of its ever ending. A captured German officer was asked by his guards, "When will the war end?" "I don't know when the war will end," the officer replied, "but I know where, and that is here. You cannot drive us back, nor can we drive you back." So it seemed to the men in the trenches, and the futility of so many lives wasted for no purpose could drive men mad.

A typical day in the trenches varied from one place to another. Usually, the day was turned upside down, with most of the work being done at night, when darkness gave greater safety to men moving about.

At dusk, after the evening meal, the command was given to "stand to." The men on duty mounted the fire step with their rifles ready. It was a drill, repeated every dusk and dawn. Usually the men fired their rifles even if there was nothing stirring on the other side. This brought an answering salvo that could result in firing all along the sector for ten or fifteen minutes. After things had quieted down, the order was given to "stand down." The real work of the night now began.

The main work in the trenches was digging. Damage done by shellfire or raid had to be repaired. New trenches were con-

LIFE IN THE TRENCHES

6

stantly being built. Water had to be pumped out of the trench, using hand pumps, and mud shoveled over the parapet. New duckboards had to be laid down on the trench floor, revetments had to be repaired, traverses reinforced. In command trenches there were sandbags, endless sandbags, to be refilled and replaced. It was dull work, backbreaking work, work carried out under danger of death at any time.

Henri Barbusse portrayed the tedium: "We stoop and crouch, and someone is scratching at the earth on his knees. Others are working full length; they toil, and turn, and turn again like men in nightmares. The earth, whose first layer was light to lift, becomes muddy and sticky; it is hard to handle, and clings to the tool like glue."

Every drop of clean water was hoarded for drinking. None was available for washing. The mud dried on the men, got wet again, got covered with more mud. There was no escape from it.

Guy Empey remembered: "The men slept in mud, washed in mud, ate mud, and dreamed mud." Fifty years later, Charles Carrington, a young British officer in the war, still shuddered at the memory of "the smell of burnt and poisoned mud . . . for months on end . . . the stink of corrupting human flesh."

The sounds of digging rang out in the night and seemed to travel for miles in the darkness. The opposing side was alert for sections of trench where men seemed to be moving about. If a noise attracted their attention, they would fire a machine-gun burst or a few artillery shells. A well-aimed shell could collapse a whole section of trench, burying the men who were working there. Then the work had to begin anew, unless there were bodies or wounded to carry away first.

Supplies for the front trenches were also brought up at night, to escape detection. Everything had to be carried by hand

A British wiring party going up to the front lines after a heavy rain.
NATIONAL ARCHIVES

through the communication trenches. This included food, ammunition, tools, duckboards, timbers for the mining parties under no-man's land, rolls of barbed wire and telephone wire, hand pumps, mail, medical supplies ... all carried by that beast of burden, the common soldier.

The communication trenches were usually narrower than the fire trench, and the constant night traffic made them crowded. A man walking through them could only see the shoulders of the man in front of him. Men moved forward by marching with their hands on the next man's shoulder. In the zigzagged trench, they might encounter a stretcher party bringing back a wounded man. The word would go back along the line to climb out of the trench to let the stretcher by. The men pulled themselves up and crouched on top, knowing that any noise could draw an enemy machine gunner's fire.

All night long, sentries watched over no-man's land and the enemy trenches. Exhausted from inadequate sleep and the backbreaking work, the sentries had to remain alert for their two-hour shifts. Out in no-man's land, both sides had men working on the barbed wire or patrolling the area. A sentry had to be sharp-eyed to tell friend from foe. If he was given orders or asked a question from the trench, he had to answer without turning or taking his eyes from no-man's land.

Penalties were severe for sentries who failed in their duty: in extreme cases, death. A sentry who fell asleep at his post could expect twenty-one days "crucifixion": for two hours a day he would be strapped in a standing position to a cart wheel or crossed posts.

An officer patrolled each section of trench all night long to make sure each man was at his post and that the work parties weren't shirking. He also checked each man for signs of the diseases that ravaged the men in the trenches.

A lonely winter night in the trenches finds a German soldier on duty. It was essential that sentries remained alert, never taking their eyes off no-man's land. LIBRARY OF CONGRESS

As a British sentry watches from the firestep, most of those around him have fallen asleep from exhaustion, sitting or lying wherever there is a bit of space. IMPERIAL WAR MUSEUM

All through the night, as a British soldier remembered, "The artillery on both sides conducted a loud-voiced argument, concussion shells played havoc with masonry, and shrapnel shells flung their deadly freight on roads where the transports hurried."

After about three in the morning, unless an attack was planned, the sector began to quiet down. Some men finished their nightly tasks and tried to catch some sleep in a darkened dugout or stretched out on the fire step. A new man noticed that veterans put their overcoats over their faces when they slept. He learned why the first time he was awakened by a rat scampering across his face.

At last, the long night began to end. The sky between the two muddy trench walls turned to gray and showed its first traces of pink. The command came once again to "stand to."

Every man jumped to his post on the fire step. This was the time of "morning hate," when both sides blasted away for another ten to fifteen minutes of intense fire. All the pent-up frustration and anger of the war was released at this time, with both sides firing at the unseen enemy that was always waiting on the other side. Most of these morning exchanges were futile expenditures of ammunition, but men were wounded and killed in them.

As suddenly as it began, morning hate subsided, and it was time for breakfast. An unspoken rule of the trenches was that both sides refrained from firing during mealtimes.

The British brought stew through communication trenches in twelve-gallon cans called "dixies." There might also be pots of "pozzy," or jam—always plum-and-apple, so that a common joke was, "When are we going to get strawberry?" Sometimes a strip of bacon was allotted to each man. Daily rations also included two cans of "bully beef," dried beef.

Then there were biscuits. One British private described these as "so hard you had to put them on a firm surface and smash them with a stone or something. I've held one in my hand and hit the sharp corner of a brick wall and only hurt my hand."

Some soldiers made "trench pudding" from the biscuits. Breaking up the biscuits, the men let them soak in water for several hours. Then they added raisins, jam, and any other available flavoring to the mix, which was boiled and allowed to harden in a sandbag. Each man then cut off a piece of the pudding and tried to force it down.

During battles or when artillery barrages kept the regular food supply from getting through, the men resorted to the canned goods called "iron rations." Nutrition experts had figured out to the calorie how much food was necessary to keep a man at fighting strength. But they had not figured out how to make the food palatable. Although fires were usually forbidden, men claimed the iron rations had to be heated to be eaten.

British emergency rations included Maconochie, which was sliced turnips and carrots in a thin broth; cans of pork and beans; a sealed can of tea, sugar, and Oxo cubes (bouillon); and finally, a slab of hard moldy cheese. British soldiers carried the cheese next to a can of whale oil they used for rifle cleaning, to give the cheese a "sardine" taste.

All drinking water had to be carried to the front by hand. It was carefully ladled out to the men, who had to make a canteen last through the day. When they were cut off from supplies, the men drank water from the pools of rain that collected in shell-holes. Even boiled, this was often poisonous. Each British soldier was also allotted a precious two ounces of rum per day.

The French and Germans had worse food than the British, by all accounts. A normal meal in the French trenches included a loaf of hard bread; kidney beans in oil; stringy and greasy canned beef that the men called *singe*, or monkey meat; pudding; coffee; and a cup of *pinard*, or red wine.

Germany became short of food as the war went on as a result of the effectiveness of the British blockade. German soldiers had to eat turnip bread, made with ground turnips and a handful of sawdust for body. Turnip stew, tubes of turnip paste (called Hindenburg fat by the troops, after their portly commander), and an occasional horsemeat stew were the staples of the German army diet after the hard winter of 1916–17. Beer was usually available to the troops.

After breakfast, the soldiers looked forward to mail call. All the armies realized the importance of the men's morale, and made sure mail was included in the daily supplies to the front lines. Men, especially officers, even ordered hampers of food by mail from stores in Paris, London, or Berlin. Newspapers arrived regularly. Wives and parents sent homemade cakes, canned goods, and candy. The men shared these food packages with each other in what they called "dinner parties."

Some of the men had no one to write to them; accordingly, it was the custom for the other men to share their letters so that everyone would have something from home to read. There were other ways a man could get mail. British newspapers published lists of "lonely soldiers." One trench veteran recalled that men whose names got on these lists received more mail than anyone else in the platoon.

Similarly, the French had *marraines,* women who volunteered to be responsible for taking care of a soldier with no relatives. Each *marraine* sent her soldier letters, food, and knitted clothing. She might even meet him when he came back on leave. Romances sometimes sprang up from such artificial introductions.

After the reading of the mail, the duties for the day began.

Better visibility made it more dangerous to move around. Enemy snipers were always watching for movement on the other side. Yet the work of repairing trenches continued. Another daytime duty was repairing the communication wires buried under the duckboards. Wireless radios were still rarely used, and cables for field telephones ran through the trench system. No matter how deeply these cables were buried, artillery shells were always destroying them and interrupting communications.

In daylight, the sentries could no longer keep a direct eye on no-man's land because to do so would make them sitting ducks for the snipers across the way. Therefore sentries used periscopes, mirrors, and iron rings with an eyehole in them to keep watch for attacks.

Lunchtime in the trenches meant more of the same food. The men wolfed it down because the continual work and strain made them hungry enough to eat anything.

In the long afternoons, men sometimes had time for personal tasks. One of these was cleaning their rifles of the ever-present dirt. French soldiers kept a cork in the barrel and wrapped a rag around the breech in a futile attempt to keep trench mud out of their weapons. During rainy spells, when nothing else worked, the men urinated in the gun barrels to clear them.

Some of the men found space in a dugout to write letters, read, or play cards. Trench humor included jokes about the endless war. An example: A man who enlisted in the British army said he signed up "for seven years." His companion shook his head. "You're lucky," he said. "I enlisted for the duration of the war."

Letters home generally told little about the true conditions in the trenches. For one thing, officers were required to read

German soldiers seeking whatever shelter they can find during an
artillery bombardment. LIBRARY OF CONGRESS

and approve the letters to make sure they didn't contain military information that could aid the enemy.

The British printed millions of postcards for the soldiers, with blanks to check opposite printed messages such as "I am quite well," "I have received your (letter, telegram, parcel)." A printed instruction warned the soldier not to add any extra messages to the card. The postcard was efficient; it also was lifeless and impersonal, contributing to the dehumanization of the war.

Other men found time to rearrange the contents of their crushingly heavy packs, looking for something to throw away. In the words of Henri Barbusse,

> The knapsack is the trunk and even the cupboard; and the old soldier is familiar with the art of enlarging it almost miraculously by the judicious disposal of his household goods and provisions. Besides the regulation and obligatory contents . . . we find a way of getting in some pots of jam, tobacco, chocolate, candles, soft-soled shoes; and even soap, a spirit lamp, some solidified spirit, and some woolen things. With the blanket, sheet, tent-cloth, trenching-tool, water bottle, and an item of the field-cooking kit—the burden gets heavier and taller and wider, monumental and crushing.

Finally, when everything else was done, there might be time to sleep. But as Guy Empey recalled:

> Try to sleep with a belt full of ammunition around you, your rifle bolt biting into your ribs, entrenching tool handle sticking into the small of your back, with a tin hat for a pillow; and feeling very damp and cold, with "cooties" boring for oil in your arm pits, the air foul from the stench of grimy human bodies and

smoke from a juicy pipe being whiffed into your nostrils.

In the late afternoon, a man smoked his last cigarette before nightfall; lit cigarettes made excellent targets at night. Dusk came; evening meal; stand to, and the "day" began again.

So it went day after day in the trenches. Death was always present. The generals had a term for the men who became trench casualties in the times between battles. They were called "wastage," and the toll of the wasted was heavy.

Snipers were a constant threat. Men were told of the futility of ducking at the sound of a rifle bullet. "You'll never hear the one that gets you," was standard advice. "Always remember that if you are going to get it, you'll get it, so don't worry."

German snipers were particularly effective. Their units served at the same section of front throughout the war, rather than being shifted from place to place as the Allies were. The German snipers thus became more familiar with the terrain and the layout of the Allied trenches.

Men who served at the front later wrote of the terrifying experience of talking to a man and having him suddenly fall with a bullet through the head. The anxiety of feeling always in jeopardy added to the strain of life in the trenches.

Another psychological strain, especially on sentries, was what the French called *cafard,* or boredom. After the dawn "stand to," there was little chance of an attack, but the sentry had to remain as vigilant as before, keeping watch on the waste and desolation of no-man's land, where dead men lay rotting on the wire and the only movement came from rats wriggling through the muck.

Rats grew huge and numerous on the western front. The corpses of men and horses that littered the ground provided more than enough food for the army of rats that were the only living things to cross no-man's land freely. They tormented the men in the trenches on both sides in their continual search for food. In the darkness of the dugouts, men could hear them gnawing away and sentries watching no-man's land were often startled in the night by rats scurrying past at eye level.

Corpses were also found inside the trenches. Men repairing walls or engaged in other digging work frequently unearthed bodies of the dead. In the heat of battle, there often wasn't time to transport bodies back through the communication trenches. Bodies were sometimes thrown over the top or sealed up in the trench walls where they stayed, forgotten, until an infantry-man's spade unearthed them. The stench that resulted was, to many, the worst of the miseries of day-to-day life in the trenches.

The foul air that filled men's nostrils came not only from decaying bodies. The unwashed bodies of the living, the pockets of poison gas that collected in shell holes and the bottom of trenches, and the burning smell of gunpowder contributed to the acrid odor that was ever present. It permeated the mud that coated everything.

The men in the trenches were universally afflicted with lice, or "cooties," as they were called. Cooties thrived in hair, clothing, and the crevices of the body. Since the men were forbidden to remove their clothing while in the front lines, all they could do was scratch and wait for their turn at the delousing stations after they were relieved. Sentries equipped themselves with eighteen-inch scratching sticks with which they claimed they could reach any part of their bodies while keeping their eyes on the opposing trench line.

Living in the trenches required latrines. Two men from each company were assigned sanitary duty. They carried back

"Danger zone" reads the sign in a German trench. In a light moment,
German soldiers apply pistol, knife, and binoculars to a hunt for cooties. NATIONAL ARCHIVES

through the communication trenches the metal cans that were sometimes used as toilets. In some trenches, a side trench was dug leading to a hole in the ground, which the men on sanitary duty had to dig deeper as required.

The latrines, in addition to the bodies of the dead and the living, attracted flies. Many soldiers recalled great clouds of shining black and green flies swarming over the trenches, particularly in summer. Captain Rommel wrote:

> One day Ensign Moricke, an especially fine soldier, visited me. I was down in my dugout, and we had to talk to each other through the shaft because there was not room for two in my warren. I told Moricke I was convinced that we were not safe from the damned flies even when we were 12 feet underground. Moricke said it was no wonder since the edge of the trench was simply black with them. He got a pick and started to dig there, and at the first swing the half-decayed, blackened arm of a Frenchman came to light. We threw chloride of lime on it and left the dead man.

Flies, cooties, rats, and the filthy men all spread diseases. Most common of these was trench foot, the result of standing in water and mud all the time with no way to dry one's feet. Boots, puttees, and layers of socks were soaked through to the skin. Trench foot resembled frostbite. The skin turned red or blue, bringing a terrible itching and peeling of the skin. If it went untreated in the filth of the trenches, it could get much worse. Gangrene could set in, requiring amputation of toes or feet.

Dampness and exposure to cold also resulted in pneumonia. The cooties spread a disease known as trench fever, for which there was no effective treatment until the last year of the war.

There were actually almost a million more Allied casualties

—severe enough to necessitate a man's removal from the line— caused by disease than by battle wounds on the western front alone in the four years of the war.

One of the sentries' duties during the day was to watch for the telltale cloud that signaled a gas attack. An empty shell casing or other alarm bell hung at the sentry's post for him to alert the trench. Usually, the men had only fifteen to twenty seconds to put on their cumbersome gas masks before the cloud arrived. The stifling atmosphere inside the mask, often reeking with chemicals meant to counteract the gas, made tearing it off a temptation.

In fact deliberately breathing the gas—at least in small doses— was one way of acquiring what the British called a "Blighty" wound, Blighty being British army slang for home. A similar expression among the German soldiers was *Heimatschuss*— "home shot." It meant a wound serious enough to send you home. The French called it *une bonne blessure* ("a good wound").

Particularly after the horrible battles of 1916, self-inflicted wounds became a serious problem in all the armies. Besides breathing gas, common attempts included shooting oneself in the hand or foot, chewing cordite (explosives in stick form: thought to be poisonous, but not fatal), sleeping in wet towels to induce pneumonia, and raising an arm or leg above trench level.

Men told grim stories of those who invited Blighty wounds. Reputedly, one British soldier stuck his arm above the trench with no response from the German lines. Then he stood on his head and waved his legs, still with no effect. Finally, he looked over the top to see what was wrong, and received a bullet through the forehead.

The desperation that led to self-inflicted injuries could also lead to insanity. Mental breakdowns were given the general name of shell shock because the continual artillery fire was the most nerve shattering of all the agonies of life in the trenches.

True shell-shock was caused by a shell landing nearby that caused a concussion that shattered a man's eardrums. The majority of shell-shock cases were in fact the result not of shelling but of extreme fatigue coupled with the anxiety of knowing that death waited at any minute.

Some men went berserk and leaped over the parapet into no-man's land and went screaming toward the unseen enemy. Those cases where the men simply collapsed and had to be brought back to hospitals were characterized by vacant stares, loose-lipped grins, and incoherent mumbling. The British army alone had eighty thousand such cases. Some men never fully recovered. There were many more cases that were not severe enough to require hospitalization. The army's attitude toward all the shell-shock victims was disapproval that they hadn't been able to "take it."

Something of the atmosphere that produced shell shock is indicated by Henri Barbusse, who relates what happened to a group of French soldiers that lost eight out of eleven men in one night.

> Barbier is killed. Saturday night it was, at eleven o'clock. He had the top of his back taken away by a shell, cut off like a razor. Besse got a bit of shell that went clean through his belly and stomach. Barthelemy and Baubex got it in the head and neck. We passed the night skedaddling up and down the trench at full speed, to dodge the showers. And little Godefroy—did you know him?—middle of his body blown away. He was emptied of blood on the spot in an instant, like a bucket kicked over. Little as he was, it was remarkable how much blood he had. It made a

stream at least fifty meters long. Gougnard got his legs cut up by one explosion. They picked him up not quite dead. I was there on duty with them. But when that shell fell I had gone to ask the time. I found my rifle, that I'd left in my place, bent double, as if someone had folded it in his hands, the barrel like a corkscrew, and half of the stock in sawdust. The smell of fresh blood was enough to bring your heart up.

Each season of the year brought its own particular kind of misery. For some, winter was the worst. The water in the trenches turned to ice and the clothing, meant for summer fighting, failed to protect against the bitter cold. The winter of 1916–17 was the coldest in Europe for decades. Men stuffed newspapers under their clothes. Rules against fire were disregarded, and the choking smoke was added to the foul air of the dugouts. Men died of suffocation while they slept as burning lanterns consumed the oxygen below ground. Men used the whale-oil-soaked rags meant for cleaning their guns as wicks for improvised torches.

Some winter clothing was issued, but it was inadequate. Gloves had no fingers so that the men could dig and pull triggers. Overcoats made from goat fur were of some help, if one could keep them dry. The Scottish regiments, which were required to wear kilts even in the trenches, got scant comfort from the wool undershorts they were given. The trench armies resembled street urchins, with rags wrapped around their feet, wool scarves bandaging their heads.

Spring came, and with it the rain and the thaws that collapsed trench walls and flooded the trenches. Sometimes flash flooding filled trenches to the top. Regulations said that each man had to change into dry socks daily to prevent trench foot, but in the trenches nothing was dry.

Waterproof capes, spread on the ground, provided a momentary dry spot. The Germans had waterproof overalls but they were in such short supply that they had to be left in the trenches for the replacement troops. The same was true of the rubber boots that the British used in the front trenches.

Heavy clothing soaked by rain became a terrible burden. The overcoats of men coming from the rain-swept Somme battlefield were weighed by some enterprising staff officer. He found some coats that weighed, wet, fifty-eight pounds; dry, they were seven pounds. The simple act of walking in the mud became a struggle, as a man's foot sunk inches deep in the muck and with each step he had to strain to pull loose. Add to that the weight of supplies that had to be carried daily through the communication trenches, the sixty-pound packs that moving troops carried with them, and it becomes remarkable that the armies functioned at all.

Summer brought with it heat, flies, quicker decay of bodies, worse odors from the living, and worst of all the great massed battles. The summer was the best time for fighting, or so the generals thought. To others, the battles were like the fields of red poppies that grew in Flanders in summer—rivers of red flooding over the landscape.

In 1914, a British medical officer said it was unwise for men to spend more than forty-eight hours in the front line. But during battles like the Somme, it was common for a battalion to spend two or three weeks there. One battalion was not relieved for fifty-one days.

Commanders at higher levels did worry that the state of exhaustion produced by continual work, little sleep, and never-ending tension would affect the fighting ability of the men. Unfortunately, there were not enough engineers to do the job of digging and repairing the trenches. Later in the war, the Brit-

Taking advantage of a rare opportunity for rest, a French *poilu* smokes his pipe. His rifle, standing at the right, is equipped for firing grenades.
NATIONAL ARCHIVES

ish added a "pioneer" battalion to each division to do heavy construction work, and imported laborers from as far away as China. The French assigned older territorial soldiers to menial labor. These adjustments lessened the load somewhat on the ordinary soldier, but his efforts remained divided between fighting and digging.

In the British army a division was assigned to hold a four-mile section of trench for two weeks. (The distance was measured "as the bullet flies"; the actual line was much longer.) Two of the division's three brigades were actually in the three lines of trenches at one time. While there, they alternated between fire trench, support trench, and "local billets." Billets were tents, huts, or abandoned buildings—usually still within reach of enemy artillery. The third brigade rested several miles behind the lines and was used for relief of the other two brigades during the two-week period of duty. After two weeks, the entire division was moved to a "rest camp" back in the rear.

The French and Germans had similar relief systems. The Germans spent more time in the trenches because reinforcement troops were spread between the eastern and western fronts.

The farther behind the fire trench, the better conditions became. Usually the first thing men did on arriving at billets was to conduct a "cootie hunt." They stripped off their clothing and picked off the lice, one by one. Since the lice laid tiny eggs in the clothing, a new crop would hatch in a few hours. Some soldiers tried to destroy the eggs by running the seams of ther clothes through a candle flame, but it was tricky to avoid burning holes in the clothes.

If the men were lucky, there might be a delousing station where their clothes could be washed in chemicals and hot water to kill the lice. The men themselves had the opportunity to soak in tubs of hot water before being issued with cleaned and pressed uniforms. Even this didn't stop the lice from returning, however.

Back of the lines it was possible for the men to purchase a little comfort and food with what they had saved from their meager pay. The Red Cross and the YMCA established canteens where the men could buy fresh eggs, canned fruit, and other food. Razors and other personal items were sold. Social and cultural events including teas, concerts, and plays were organized by the charitable groups that operated these canteens. A division might set up its own canteen where the men could buy liquor and tobacco.

Behind the lines, at the rest camps, a favorite amusement was the staging of short plays written by the men. One of them portrayed the war still going on in 1967, with the grandchildren of the original soldiers moving up to take their places in the trenches.

In some places, the men published their own newspapers. These generally included humorous articles, such as this advertisement for *Flammenwerfers* (German flamethrowers) in the *Wipers Times—Salient News:*

Has Your Boy a Mechanical Turn of Mind? Yes!
Then buy him a
FLAMMENWERFER
Instructive—Amusing
Both young and old enjoy
This natty little toy.
Guaranteed Absolutely Harmless
Thousands Have Been Sold

In the French army, more serious newspapers circulated

Australian soldiers resting in dugouts near Ypres. Card playing was one of the men's few pastimes in the trenches. This dugout is particularly well reinforced, with brick ceilings and heavy timbers for support. AUSTRALIAN WAR MEMORIAL

among the men. As the war grew more costly, political groups agitated in France for a negotiated peace. Part of their campaign was to convince the troops that their lives were being wasted in a useless effort.

For a man who wanted to drown his sorrows in something stronger than fruit juice, there was usually an *estaminet* near the billets. These were little cafés run by French villagers, behind both German and Allied lines. Wine, beer, and liquor were served in an atmosphere that took the men away from the rigors of military discipline.

Gambling and sex were two other occupations of men behind the lines. Any *estaminet* or army canteen had its games of chance, some sponsored by enterprising soldiers, some by the *estaminet* owner. The British were fond of "house," which was similar to bingo. Piquet was one of numerous card games popular among the French soldiers. The Germans liked skittles, a miniature bowling game.

Houses of prostitution thrived behind the lines. Official attitudes toward prostitution varied. Among the British, it was widely believed that the men could not endure total abstention from sex. On the other hand, moral pressure from the home front and the risk of spreading venereal disease among the men caused army commanders to make occasional attempts at ruling houses of prostitution "off limits." These prohibitions were seldom seriously enforced.

Not that life behind the lines ever consisted merely of relaxation and fun. Far from it, for not only were the army commanders anxious to preserve discipline, but there really was a need for more training and more work. Beginning on the second morning back, there was daily inspection of the men, and all were expected to have thrown off the fatigue of the trenches, be clean shaven, and properly attired.

The men behind the lines were used to repair railroad links, build better billets, and transport supplies back to the front. Empey explained, "In France they call them rest billets, because while in them Tommy works seven days a week and on the eighth day of the week he is given 24 hours on his own." "Tommy" is the British equivalent of G. I. Joe: Tommy Atkins. German soldiers were known as "Fritz" and the Frenchmen were *poilus,* or hairy ones, a term of affection.

Training camps behind the lines were often rigorous and even brutal. Conditions were so harsh at the British camp at Etaples, known to the men as "the Bull Ring," that the soldiers rioted in 1918 and seemed on the verge of mutiny. A soldier recalled meeting men on their way back to the front with wounds that had not healed. They told him they would rather go back "to get away from the Bull Ring."

The trenches exerted a fascination for the men who survived them. It went beyond the experience of danger and death. Those who fought in the trenches were set apart from men who were never there. It was not an experience that could be explained; if you were there, you shared in it. That was enough.

All who wrote about the experience have tried to express the comradeship and love that was felt among the men in the trenches. An English soldier wrote, "The love that grows quickly and perhaps artificially when men are together against life and death has a peculiar quality. Death that cuts it off does not touch the emotions at all, but works right in the soul of you." Men spoke of those who had "gone West," or been killed, in the same way that they spoke of a live person who was not present.

Erich Maria Remarque, who served in the German army, expressed something of the same feeling: "It is a great brotherhood, which to a condition of life arising out of the midst of danger, adds something of the good-fellowship of the folk-song, of the feeling of solidarity of convicts, and of the desperate loyalty to one another of men condemned to death."

Religion generally was held in contempt by the soldiers who had read the uninformed propaganda spouted by religious leaders at home. Chaplains of the Church of England did not go in the front lines, although some Roman Catholic priests won respect by coming to the front and even going to no-man's land to rescue wounded. In the French army, priests were drafted to serve like any other able-bodied male.

The comradeship of the trenches was also an alienation from the rest of society. Those who went home on leave felt suddenly alone, cut off, and actually yearned to return. The mystical feeling of comradeship sometimes even included the enemy. Men realized that the unseen enemies on the other side also shared their experiences. The prisoners that had been taken into the lines showed that the enemy was a man just like everybody else, despite what the propaganda from home said.

This attitude led to occasional fraternization between the opposing troops, to the consternation of the generals. Sometimes truces were called for practical reasons, such as collecting the wounded and burying the dead. As time went on, it seemed sensible to some units to call truces for other work duties, such as fixing the barbed wire. Whenever officers discovered such impromptu truces, they were obliged to demand that fighting be resumed. Some officers ignored their instructions, and let the truces proceed.

In the evenings, soldiers who found themselves with a free moment used to improvise musical instruments. Someone might play a harmonica; others sang. Since the trenches were usually within earshot of each other, the other side sometimes joined in the singing.

French cooks and kitchen police preparing soup to be carried in cans to the men in the trenches. NATIONAL ARCHIVES

At Christmas, 1914, the fraternization was widespread, with officers and men alike meeting in no-man's land to exchange cigarettes and souvenirs, take photographs of each other, show pictures of their families, and compare news accounts of the war. Christmas trees were set up and decorated in no-man's land. In some parts of the line, the Christmas fraternization lasted till New Year's Day. The generals issued strict orders that such a thing must never happen again. In 1915, when it occurred again on a smaller scale, officers of offending units were court-martialed.

But we can imagine the scene as the soldiers tentatively raised their heads above the parapet and climbed gingerly into rat-infested no-man's land. Suddenly there, coming from the other trenches, picking their way through the barbed wire and the corpses were other mud-caked men, tired, hungry, swarming with lice. They held out their hands to their mirror images.

Until 1916, the French had carried the Allied burden of the war on the western front. France defended the greater part of the line, had many more men on the front than the British, and suffered greater numbers of casualties.

The high casualties were due in part to the unswerving belief of the French general staff in the doctrine of attack. Through 1915, Joffre struck again and again in the Artois and Champagne area. By the end of 1915, France had lost fifty percent of the officers in the regular army and the number of French dead almost equaled the total that Britain would lose in the entire war.

The Germans had suffered too. Falkenhayn, the German commander, decided in December, 1915, on a plan to knock France out of the war. With France gone, he reasoned, Britain would have lost its strongest ally, and would stop fighting.

Falkenhayn chose a place to attack that he knew the French would *have* to defend. The city of Verdun, ringed with fortresses, had been a citadel since the time of the Romans. In the Franco-Prussian War of 1870, it had been the last French stronghold to surrender. In 1914, it had helped hold the line against Germany while Joffre shifted troops to the Battle of the Marne.

Falkenhayn knew that the French would fight ferociously to hold Verdun. That was what he wanted, for his primary objec-

MUTINY   7

tive was not to capture the city, but to "bleed France white" in a protracted defense against the constant pressure of German troops. Falkenhayn gave the Verdun offensive the code name *Gericht*, or "Place of Execution." The attack was planned to begin February 12, 1916.

Joffre had no real faith in the defensive strength of the forts surrounding Verdun. He had seen what the German "Big Berthas" had done to the Belgian forts at Liège, and presumed that the French forts would fall quickly in the face of a similar artillery attack. In 1915, needing artillery and troops for attacks in other parts of the front, Joffre had stripped the forts of their guns and shifted men away from the Verdun salient, which had remained quiet since 1914.

There were those in the French army who saw the threat of a German attack at Verdun. A Lieutenant Colonel Emile Driant wrote to the civilian leadership, warning them of the state of Verdun's defenses. Proper trench lines had not been dug, discipline was lax, and there were early indications that the Germans were planning an attack.

In response, Joffre denounced "soldiers under my command bringing before the government . . . complaints or protests concerning the execution of my orders . . . calculated to disturb profoundly the spirit of discipline in the Army. . . ." It was not until late in January, 1916, that Joffre ordered the defenses of Verdun to be reinforced; by then, it was almost too late.

The assault on Verdun was assigned to the German Fifth Army, under the command of the kaiser's eldest son, Crown Prince Wilhelm. The crown prince was not aware of Falkenhayn's plan: to wage a prolonged battle of attrition. His own plans were to capture the citadel as quickly as possible. He urged that the attack be launched from both sides of the river Meuse, to the north and to the east of Verdun.

Some of the devastation around Verdun. The bombardment there was the heaviest in the war up to that time. Whole villages were wiped out, leaving only a few walls and shell craters. FRENCH EMBASSY PRESS AND INFORMATION DIVISION, NEW YORK

But Falkenhayn ordered that the attack come from the east bank only. It was to be an intense attack, concentrated on a front eight miles wide for which the Germans brought up fourteen hundred cannons, including thirteen 420-millimeter (16.5-inch) siege guns. The Germans built huge concrete dugouts, called *Stollen*, underneath their trenches as jumping-off places for troops that were to storm the trenches in front of the French forts. The purpose of the *Stollen* was to act as a protected place for troops during the opening counterbarrage by the French. Some of the underground *Stollen* were so large they could hold half a battalion.

On the morning of the twelfth, a blizzard raged around Verdun, making it impossible for the German artillery to sight their targets. The attack had to be postponed. The bad weather continued for nine more days.

The *Stollen* lacked facilities to hold all the men there overnight. Each day the attack was postponed most of the men had to march through the snow to their billets, some of which were seven miles to the rear. Each day they came back to wait for the attack.

The air grew foul in the *Stollen*; tempers were short. Freezing water seeped into the huge dugouts; there was a shortage of pumps. Men waited knee deep in water for the order to attack to come. Days of waiting preyed on their nerves. Rumors spread that something had gone wrong, that there were spies in the trenches, that there was to be no attack.

Finally, on the twenty-first, the weather cleared and the German bombardment began just before dawn. "We had never experienced anything like it," wrote a French survivor.

> Shells of all calibers kept raining on our sector. The trenches had disappeared, filled with earth. . . . The air was unbreathable. Our blinded, wounded, crawl-

ing and shouting soldiers kept falling on top of us and died splashing us with their blood. It was living hell.

For concentrated firepower, there never had been anything like the German barrage. It was the ultimate expression of the theory that massive force of armament and artillery could achieve an objective. More than 10 million shells fell on the defenses of Verdun that one day.

The barrage continued all morning, falling from the front line of trenches all the way back to Verdun itself, some twenty miles from the German lines. At noon the bombardment suddenly stopped. Expecting the attack to follow, the surviving French troops emerged from what was left of their dugouts. Now the German artillery spotters and aircraft could see which sections of trench had withstood the shelling. The barrage then resumed on the sections of trench that still held defenders.

The Germans isolated the French front-line trenches by using a box barrage that kept reinforcements, supplies, and messages from reaching the sector marked for attack. Special attention was given to knocking out French artillery, machine guns, and strongpoints in this sector.

The advance of the German troops began at 4:00 that afternoon. Despite reports from scouting patrols that nothing was left alive in the French trenches, the Germans advanced in small groups, seeking cover where they could find it, and only attacking those parts of the French trench line that offered little or no resistance.

After German troops overwhelmed the weaker spots in the line, the work of "consolidation" began. Reinforcements were moved up, strongpoints still held by the French were bombarded with accurate, close-range mortars, and the Germans moved toward the forts of Verdun. By February 24, the Ger-

French soldiers in the trenches at Verdun. The trenches here had been
in poor condition before the battle, because previously it had been a
"quiet sector." UNITED PRESS INTERNATIONAL PHOTO

mans had penetrated to a depth of three and a half miles. The French pulled back, shortening their own line to try and strengthen it for the next German thrust.

The worst blow to French pride came on February 25 with the fall of Fort Douaumont. Joffre's calculations about the forts had been wrong. They had stood up to the German bombardment. But unfortunately, their garrisons had been reduced to only a few soldiers. At Douaumont, a single German company walked unopposed into the fort after the trenches in front of it had been cleared.

The fall of Douaumont was acclaimed in Germany as a great victory. The attention of the German people was now fixed on Verdun, waiting for the imminent fall of the city to the crown prince's troops. Just as resolute was public opinion in France, which demanded that Verdun be held. Joffre named General Henri Pétain to command the defenders of Verdun. French reinforcements swarmed toward Verdun by train and motor transport. The motto of the defending troops was *Ils ne passeront pas*—They shall not pass—and the words electrified France.

Pétain arrived on February 26 and set to work. The immediate task was to strengthen and defend the one supply road that was left open. The French defenders renamed it *La Voie Sacrée*—the Sacred Way—and kept it open throughout the furious German artillery barrages. The road had to be constantly strengthened and rebuilt to accommodate round-the-clock traffic. At the height of its use, trucks carrying troops and supplies passed every thirteen seconds. During the first week in March, 190,000 soldiers traveled along *La Voie Sacrée* into Verdun.

Because Falkenhayn had not permitted the crown prince's army to attack from the north, Pétain was able to assemble artillery on the west bank of the Meuse. As the Germans approached from the east, they were caught in artillery fire from their flank. Slowly the attack ground to a halt, and on February 28, the Germans began to establish a trench line to protect themselves from the artillery.

On March 6, the crown prince launched a new offensive, this time on the left bank of the Meuse, north of the city. His objective was the French artillery on a ridge known as Mort Homme —Dead Man. The old pattern of the western front appeared again: a thunderous artillery barrage followed by an attack that gained a few hundred yards, then bogged down again. Fighting around Mort Homme produced some of the heaviest casualties of the war.

A French Jesuit priest, who was serving in the infantry, wrote of the fighting at Mort Homme:

> The most solid nerves cannot resist for long; blood mounts to the head; fever burns the body and the nerves, exhausted, become incapable of reacting ... one has no longer even the strength to cover oneself with one's pack as protection—and one scarcely still has the strength to pray.

Each day, the Germans clawed their way a few yards closer to Verdun, but at a far heavier price than Falkenhayn had expected. At the end of March, the Germans had suffered 82,000 casualties to France's 89,000. Heavy fighting was still going on to the east of the city. The Germans were now in the trap Falkenhayn had planned for the French.

After almost three months of fighting, the Germans took Mort Homme. But Verdun still stood in French hands. All around Verdun the landscape resembled the face of the moon— pockmarked with shell craters, burned black, and only a few craggy stumps to mark the places where forests had stood. The

P.E.L. German Dead
Dead Man's Hill

Aftermath of Verdun. German bones unearthed on *Mort Homme*— Dead Man's Hill. LIBRARY OF CONGRESS

stench of the decaying bodies that lay half-buried in the rubble grew worse as the weather became warmer. Wiped out completely in the fighting were a number of small French villages that had been in the paths of the armies. An American pilot serving with the French flew over Verdun and saw around it:

> that sinister brown belt, a strip of murdered nature. It seems to belong to another world. Every sign of humanity has been swept away. The woods and roads have vanished like chalk wiped from a blackboard; of the villages nothing remains but gray smears.

Pétain felt keenly the horror of the tremendous toll of bloodshed—too keenly, Joffre thought. In April, Joffre promoted Pétain to commander of the army group that included Verdun. General Robert Nivelle was named to head the army actually manning the defenses at Verdun.

Falkenhayn was by now convinced that the Germans were wasting men at Verdun, but Germany expected a victory. The crown prince had become identified with the battle and royal prestige was at stake. In June, the German bombardment resumed, this time on a three-mile front that centered on Fort Vaux, which was with Fort Souville the last of the great forts barring the Germans' approach east of the city.

The French garrison sent to hold Fort Vaux resisted with superhuman courage. The Germans surrounded the fort, subjecting it to intense fire. Only the French machine guns kept back the attack. Each night, the defenders of the fort could hear the digging of the Germans widening the communications trenches to bring up more men for the next day's attack. Again and again the Germans threw themselves against the fort's defenses.

The defenders held fast, till their water supply gave out. In the last three days of the battle, each man was allotted half a glass of water. The fort surrendered on June 7.

The fall of Fort Vaux was a serious blow to the French. Every available man was now set to work digging trenches in front of Verdun.

In late May Joffre had approached Haig, pleading for the British to start the offensive at the Somme, to take pressure off the French at Verdun. Haig suggested August 15 as a date. Joffre said the French army might have ceased to exist by that time. Haig promised a British attack on July 1. Verdun would have to hold out till then.

On June 23, the Germans introduced their "green cross" artillery shells at Verdun. These shells were filled with phosgene gas, ten times as deadly as the gas used at the beginning of the war. The green-cross shells knocked out the French artillery crews and the Germans advanced on Verdun, with only the trench lines now blocking their way.

Then on June 24, the bombardment at the Somme began. The Germans shifted some of their army to prevent a breakthrough there. The battle for Verdun was over. The French promise had been kept: they did not pass. The cost, however, was 315,000 French casualties and 281,000 Germans.

Nivelle and Charles Mangin, a close subordinate, were not satisfied with a stalemate. All through September and early October, shells for the French guns were transported to Verdun. Nivelle's specialty was artillery, and he planned to use a new kind of artillery barrage to retake the forts, beginning with Douaumont.

The creeping artillery barrage had been used by General Congreve's XIII Corps at the Somme. It relied on precise coordination of artillery and infantry. As the infantry advanced, the artillery fire moved just ahead of it, saturating the defending trenches with shellfire. There was no pause in the bombardment to allow the Germans to come up from their dugouts and repel the attackers. By the time they emerged, the infantry would be in the trenches with grenades and bayonets.

On October 18, the French counterattack began. French 400-millimeter (16-inch) shells pounded into the fort for three days. The Germans were compelled to withdraw all but a tiny garrison from the fort itself. Other defenders huddled in the trenches between the fort and the French trench line. Nivelle halted the barrage on the twenty-second, and repeated the trick that the Germans had played back in February. As the survivors came above ground, French artillery spotters marked their positions and bombarded them for two days more.

On the twenty-fourth Nivelle's creeping barrage began. Nivelle's tactics were a huge success. German prisoners were captured in their dugouts. Douaumont and Fort Vaux were retaken. By mid-December, much of the ground taken by the Germans to the east of Verdun had been recaptured.

In the fighting at Verdun, Pétain instituted a system of rotation that brought troops from all along the front into Verdun. During the battle, more than 70 percent of the French army participated in the fighting. None of them would ever forget it. The soldiers were tired of the war, tired of blood being shed needlessly over the same ground year after year, tired of life in the trenches.

In December, 1916, Nivelle was named commander in chief of the French armies. Nivelle was a charismatic figure, impressive looking and persuasive in speech. He rallied the army, assured the French government that he had a plan that would ensure victory the following year, and even persuaded the British prime minister to subordinate Haig and the BEF to his command for the coming offensive.

When Nivelle revealed the details of his plan for ending the war, there was consternation among the French leaders. He planned yet another assault on the German salient between Artois and Champagne. Nivelle reassured his doubters that this attack was to be different.

Nivelle planned a sudden attack in great force, using a brief artillery barrage beforehand to gain the element of surprise. The creeping barrage that had been used with such success at Douaumont and Vaux would be employed all along the front to sweep the troops through the German lines.

Nivelle assembled nearly a million men to take part in the main French attack. To the north of the salient, the British would launch a major attack at Arras a week before the French, to draw the German troops away from the area of the main thrust. Nivelle was so confident of success, he promised to achieve a major breakthrough within forty-eight hours after the attack began.

Events conspired against Nivelle. In Germany, Falkenhayn had been replaced by the dual command of Hindenburg and Ludendorff. On visiting the Somme area after taking command, Hindenburg and Ludendorff ordered a halt to the German counteroffensives there and a reduction of forces holding the front line. They reasoned that an impregnable defensive position was the key to wearing down the Allied armies in the west.

They set to work constructing an entirely new trench line from Lens to Reims. This would reduce the salient where Joffre had attacked in 1915 and where Nivelle was planning a new attack.

The new line was called the Siegfried Line by the Germans and the Hindenburg Line by the Allies. The Germans constructed it several miles to the rear of the original line and

A French soldier meets death in an assault on German positions in
Champagne. NATIONAL ARCHIVES

were able to pick their sites and build strong fortifications. The main front-line defenses were heavily constructed pillboxes, or concrete machine-gun shelters. Pillboxes were often situated behind barbed wire or in flooded areas to make it difficult for advancing infantry to overrun them. The pillboxes were scattered over a depth of three to four miles.

The second line, out of range of Allied artillery, contained the greater part of the troops manning the line. They stood ready to counterattack against any group of attackers who had broken through the first defense line.

When the Germans pulled back to the Siegfried Line, they left scorched earth behind them. They burned or destroyed anything that would be valuable to the Allies, including villages, farmhouses, and roads. They also left mines and booby traps for Allied soldiers advancing over the same ground. When the Germans withdrew in late February, Haig suggested that a new plan of attack be prepared. Nivelle refused, insisting that the original plan was still sound.

The Germans had a good idea of what Nivelle was planning. They had noted his use of the creeping barrage at Verdun. Nivelle himself compromised the secrecy of his plan by letting it be known to too many subordinates too early. A trench raid by the Germans actually managed to capture an officer who had a copy of the plan. Moreover, it was the talk of Paris for weeks before the battle, reaching ears sympathetic to the Germans.

On April 9, Haig's offensive began on schedule. His men fought bravely, notably the Canadians in capturing Vimy Ridge. Some of the British forces advanced three and a half miles that first day. But once more, the attack slowed. Haig continued to keep the Germans away from Nivelle's offensive. By late May, when the attack petered out, the British had suffered another 150,000 casualties; Germans, 100,000.

On April 16, Nivelle's men attacked in force between Reims and Soissons. Nivelle's last message to the army was: "The hour has come! Confidence! Courage! Vive la France!"

Nivelle's choice of a place of attack proved to be unwise. The Germans in most areas of the front occupied heavily fortified trenches on ridges overlooking the French positions. The main thrust of the Nivelle offensive was toward the Chemin des Dames Ridge, along which the French succeeded in taking six positions. Even so, French casualties in the first three weeks of the fighting are estimated to have been 187,000; Germans, 163,000. And there was no breakthrough.

Nivelle had promised more. On May 15, he was relieved of his command. Pétain replaced him, taking command of an army that had cracked. On April 29, French soldiers began to mutiny.

Details of the mutinies remain in secret French military archives to this day. How many men participated, how many were court-martialed, how many men executed, are not known precisely. The causes are also in dispute. Various groups within France were urging an end to the fighting. Even within the government there were pacifists. The minister of the interior refused to move to stop the flow of pacifistic pamphlets that were being circulated among the troops by civilian agitators. France, a country partly occupied by foreign troops, had known the horrors of war for too long and was disillusioned.

The soldiers did not need pamphlets to tell them the war was going badly. Nor did they need to be told that trench life was miserable and that the carnage of battle was terrifying and wasteful. The soldiers had specific complaints about food, medical care, leave, and even conditions at home. Stories about "shirkers" at home making money off the war were widely circulated.

Some of the complaints were well founded. In the Nivelle offensive, the understaffed French medical corps prepared for fifteen thousand wounded; in the first two days there were over 100,000. Wounded men lay where they fell. In the rear of the French lines, two hundred wounded men captured a hospital train and commandeered it away from the front. In one military hospital, with thirty-five hundred beds, there were four thermometers.

French soldiers on their way to the front began to bleat like sheep as they marched, reminding each other they were being led to slaughter. Signs were posted on the walls of billets, proclaiming, "Down with the war! Death to those who are responsible!" Soldiers ordered to return to the front rioted and some assaulted their commanders. The mutiny spread like a virus. Troops in rebellion marched in formation to the next battalion to urge their comrades to join them in laying down their arms. Men refused the order to go over the top.

In Paris, the government was divided. The Chamber of Deputies, in secret session, heard left-wing members question the ability of France to continue fighting. In the streets of Paris, militant *midinettes* (working women) paraded in support of the mutiny. During May and June there were over 170 work stoppages in war plants in support of the mutineers.

The mutiny grew. By June, half the divisions of the French army were openly insubordinate. No one could be sure if troops would obey orders to go to the front. The mutineers claimed they would hold their places in the line against German attacks, but would not participate in any more offensives. They demanded that the government negotiate an armistice with the Germans immediately.

Fortunately for France, the Germans never tested the ability of the mutineers to defend their lines. Absolute secrecy was

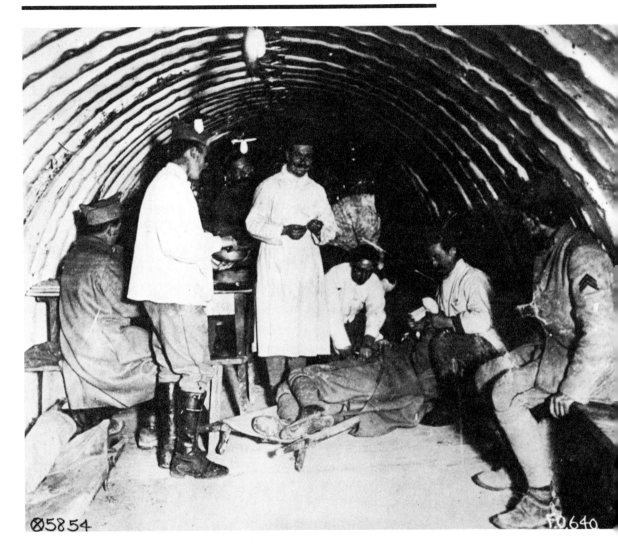

A French bombproof hospital underground near the fighting lines in the Aisne district. Under a few electric lights, doctors tried to perform emergency surgery to save lives. Part of the discontent in the French army was due to inadequate medical support. NATIONAL ARCHIVES

maintained, and the Germans did not realize the extent of the mutiny until it was over.

Into this situation stepped Pétain. For once the right leader was found. Pétain adopted a policy of sympathy to the grievances of the men coupled with severity toward the leaders of the mutiny. He ordered improvements in the living conditions of the men. The food was upgraded. Regular leaves and adequate transportation were arranged so that soldiers could spend their leave time at home. Pétain organized canteens behind the lines, ordered the construction of better latrine and bath facilities, and demanded the upgrading of the medical corps.

At the same time, Pétain was ruthless in his punishment of the leaders of the mutiny. One estimate has fifty-five officially executed. Summary courts-martial levied punishments on many more. Rumors, never confirmed, told of whole units being mowed down by loyal soldiers with machine guns.

Above all, however, Pétain promised a real change in the use of soldiers' lives. "Lavish with steel, stingy with blood" became the slogan of the French army. He visited over one hundred divisions personally, telling the men there would be no more blind offensives. "We must wait for the Americans and the tanks," Pétain said, referring to the United States' declaration of war on Germany in April, 1917, and the hoped-for weapon that was designed to break through the trench lines without costly losses of men.

The French army believed Pétain. By the end of June, the worst of the mutiny was over. Later in the year, the French army carried out a few limited offensives successfully. In one of them, Mort Homme was recaptured. The French army was a fighting unit again.

The waste and devastation of trench warfare were nowhere more apparent than in the blasted strip of land called no-man's land. Rotting corpses lay tangled in barbed wire. Shell holes filled with fetid water pocked the ground. The muck which had been soaked with rain and churned up by shellfire could swallow up a man who stepped into a soft spot. No-man's land became the symbol for the hopelessness of the war.

The terrain of no-man's land had been created by the continual artillery fire. The vegetation of the area was blasted away with the exception of a few trunks where trees had stood. Sometimes where the area between the trenches was particularly wide, ruins of villages remained in the center.

The millions of shells created huge craters that gave the land the appearance of the face of the moon. During attacks these craters were used as places of refuge for soldiers crossing no-man's land. Ducking into a crater would be an unnerving experience—a soldier never knew if he would find himself face to face with a friend, an enemy, or a dead man. Men pinned down in shell holes for hours sometimes shared their hiding places with the mangled bodies of their friends.

When men recalled no-man's land after the war, their most vivid memory was of the barbed wire. The barbed wire took on the appearance of a living thing that grew where trees and flowers had been. It symbolized the sterility and mechanization

NO-MAN'S LAND 8

of the war. At first only a single strand of it had been set up in front of each trench. Tin cans and other bits of scrap metal were hung on it to provide an alarm in case of an enemy patrol brushing against it in the night. This first strand was usually placed just beyond a grenade's throw from the trench, so that enemy raiders couldn't throw a quick grenade and then retreat.

But as the defensive positions hardened, more strands of barbed wire were laid down to ensnare attacking troops. At night, both sides sent out wiring parties to put up more wire, to repair wire, or to cut wire in preparation for an attack. Wire cutters and thick gloves were part of the soldier's basic equipment. A strand of wire had to be gripped tightly while it was cut, to avoid the telltale "twang" that could attract enemy fire.

In the sectors where no-man's land narrowed to a few yards, wiring parties from opposing armies had to work almost side by side, and adopted a "live-and-let-live" policy while they were working. Jokes spread that both sides shared the same mallets for driving the stakes on which the wire was attached.

A wiring party working alone was in more danger than if an enemy party was present, since the enemy's machine guns and artillery were then free to fire at any noise they heard. A dropped pair of wire cutters or the twang of a wire not cut properly could cost the lives of an entire patrol.

Night in no-man's land also saw men at listening posts, men on patrol, and occasional raiding parties. Aside from attacks, these details brought the only contact with the enemy. Men with blackened faces and all identification removed met in ghostly and brutal encounters.

Narrow trenches called "saps" were dug out from the main trenches into no-man's land. These saps could be used to launch a surprise raid, but more commonly they served as listening posts. Here two or three soldiers squatted in the darkness or flattened themselves against the ground. They listened for sounds of underground digging that might signal the approach of an enemy tunnel designed for mining the trenches. The sound of more men moving about in the front-line trenches might signal the preparations for an attack, as would the sound of an enemy cutting his wire. The location of a sniper or new machine-gun post might be determined by men at listening posts. Information as to what enemy units occupied the opposing trenches was also valuable.

Duty at the listening stations was arduous and nerve-racking. A breeze could set the barbed wire shivering, or a passing rat could dislodge a clod of earth. The least sound in the night made men tense, wondering if it were an enemy patrol about to stumble over the side of the trench.

Both sides sent night patrols out into no-man's land to assert their control of the area. Patrols were sent to observe the organization and activity of enemy trenches, but normally they learned little that would justify the risks they took.

Both sides could light up the night sky with flares, star shells, and Very lights that were fired from long pistols. The shells could reach a height of sixty feet and had a range of fifty to seventy-five yards fired straight out into no-man's land. On hitting the ground they exploded, throwing calcium lights in a radius of ten to fifteen yards. There was also a variety of star shell known as the parachute that exploded at a height of sixty feet and illuminated a large area. These flares added an element of evil beauty to the horror of night chores. Men on patrol were safe if the flare landed between them and the enemy trench but if they landed behind the patrol, their silhouettes could be seen by enemy riflemen. If a parachute shell illumi-

A German soldier cutting the barbed wire to allow a raiding party through on the Aisne front. NATIONAL ARCHIVES

An American soldier caught in the wire was an easy target from the German trenches. LIBRARY OF CONGRESS

nated the landscape, a man caught in no-man's land learned that his best tactic was to freeze. It was movement that attracted the eye of enemy snipers.

Robert Graves described a British patrol that he went on, accompanied by an experienced sergeant. They carried pistols, blacked their faces, and covered their knees with cut-off socks. (Summer uniforms included short pants in the British army.) They crawled on all fours, going ten yards at a time, moving slowly. At each ten-yard interval, they would lie quietly and watch, "glaring at the darkness until it began turning round and round."

They crossed through the British and German barbed wire, tearing their clothes but not getting caught. "Once I snatched my fingers in horror from where I had planted them on the slimy body of an old corpse," wrote Graves. Finally, he and the sergeant crawled to within five yards of the "sap-head"—the German listening post. They watched it for twenty minutes, waiting for signs of movement. Finally, with drawn revolvers, they slipped into the information post and to their relief found it empty. In all, Graves reports, it took them more than two hours to crawl a total of 200 yards. They were looking for anything left behind in the sap that might be useful to military intelligence.

German patrols were usually larger—five or six men under the command of a sergeant. When patrols ran across each other in the darkness, a silent, desperate battle followed. Bowie knives were typical weapons of Germans on patrol, while the British enlisted men preferred "coshes," or weighted clubs. Firing rifles or pistols in no-man's land was likely to draw fire from both opposing trenches.

If an enemy soldier was caught on patrol, he was usually

killed to keep him from sounding an alarm. If he was wearing insignia, they were taken for army intelligence, which found them valuable to know which units were serving in certain sectors. For this reason, most patrols removed their insignia before they went out.

Still more dangerous were the trench raids. These varied in size from small parties that dropped a grenade or two in the opposing trenches and returned, up to large raiding parties intended to capture and hold part of the enemy line. The more frequent smaller raids were used to spread fear and break the morale of the enemy. Larger raids might inflict casualties, take prisoners, and destroy parts of trenches and fortifications.

Guy Empey describes a raid of twenty men in which he and the others were caught in the glow of a Very light and fired on by Germans in the front trenches. The patrol scattered, with only one man returning unhurt. In the darkness, some men became confused and crawled toward the enemy trenches. The only sure way to tell where one was was that on the British side barbed wire hung on wooden stakes, while the Germans used metal ones.

Erwin Rommel described trench raids with a bit more zest:

> The nights were really exciting. Hand grenade battles went on for hours along a broad front and became so confused that we never knew whether or not the enemy had broken through at some place or had worked his way behind our front line.

Larger raids might be accompanied by gas attacks, artillery bombardment, underground explosions set by sappers, and front-line mortar fire. A useful type of barrage for large raids proved to be the box barrage, which isolated an area of trench

British soldiers in the Passchendaele area walking across the morass of a shell-blackened area. The raised plank walk was called "duckboards," and was often used to line the bottoms of trenches. The next rain usually washed them under the mud. IMPERIAL WAR MUSEUM

so that reinforcements could not get to it. The box barrage was accompanied by mortar fire directly on the front-line trench under attack.

By the time the artillery began firing, the trench raiding party was already in no-man's land, cutting their way through barbed wire. Theirs was a dangerous position because of the numerous "shorts" that the artillery fired.

The raiders, crawling on their stomachs, got as close as possible to the enemy trench. Alerted by the artillery barrage, enemy soldiers were by now scanning the darkness anxiously. Mortar fire was supposed to keep them under cover, but it often was not accurate.

Usually the attackers announced their presence with grenades lobbed into the trench from the darkness. These had to be accurately thrown, since a grenade that landed on the parapet was more likely to send bits of shrapnel flying toward the raiding party than on the trench below.

Jumping into a darkened trench where a bayonet or a Bowie knife might be waiting was the next step. There was no way to look before you leaped, either.

Some raids took prisoners for interrogation. Captured documents from raids also proved helpful to army intelligence, as in the case of the captured plans of the Nivelle offensive.

Although these raids sometimes resulted in tactical advantages, they frequently resulted in the loss of most or all of the attack party. As disillusionment over the war spread, line officers and men began to feel that trench raids were an exercise in showing the enemy that he shouldn't be too complacent. For such limited results, front-line soldiers couldn't see that the risk was worth it. As a result, in most sectors after 1916, trench raids were carried out with something less than zeal.

Beneath no-man's land there was still more activity. The

miners, or "sappers," were engaged in tunneling directly under the enemy positions. The objective of the tunneling was to place explosives, or mines, under the enemy trenches. This tactic was first used by the Germans on December 20, 1914, when they blew up half a mile of British trenches near Festubert. Indian soldiers manning the trenches panicked and ran as the ground erupted beneath their feet. The British and French responded by organizing their own mining operations and by establishing listening posts to provide early warning of advancing German tunnels.

The first sappers in the British army were experienced tunnel diggers who had worked on subways and railway tunnels in Britain. Many of these men were over the maximum induction age of thirty-five. As a group, they were as colorful and devil-may-care as the celebrated pilots who made up the early air forces of the warring nations.

In preparing a mining operation, the first step was to dig a shaft straight down to about thirty feet. Later in the war, the tunnels were dug much deeper to avoid countermining operations. Ladders enabled men to move in and out of the shaft, at the bottom of which horizontal tunnels were dug toward enemy lines.

All the dirt removed in tunneling operations had to be shoveled into sandbags and carried to the surface. The telltale sign of fresh earth from deep underground—often a different color from earth near the surface—would otherwise have been spotted by scouting planes and alerted the enemy to sapping operations.

Equipment was usually limited to picks and shovels because heavy equipment could be spotted from the air. Digging was done by candlelight, and the ventilation in the tunnels was sometimes so bad that the candles went out. Men collapsed from lack of oxygen and had to be carried to the surface.

There was a constant danger of cave-ins, more so than in civilian tunneling work, where a site could be chosen for stability and tunnel reinforcements openly brought in. In the trench tunnels, timbers were used to shore up the walls and ceiling under no-man's land. In some areas, notably around Ypres, the tunnels were always sinkholes of ooze and seepage because of the swamplike conditions.

Sometimes both sides were tunneling simultaneously, with the crews driving deeper underground in an attempt to undercut the other side. Each group tried to plant explosives that would collapse the enemy's tunnels. Mines used for this purpose were called *camouflets*, meaning figuratively in French an insult, and were placed as close to the enemy tunnel system as possible. Because of this danger, the standard system was composed of two parallel tunnels connected by lateral passages that provided a means of escape and ventilation in the event of a cave-in or explosion. Other tunnels branched out from the main system to serve as underground listening posts.

On occasion, two opposing groups of tunnelers would break into each other's tunnel system and underground battles fought with shovels and pistols would ensue.

The largest mining operation of the war took place under the Messines Ridge, a German stronghold east of the Ypres salient. The British began planning this operation at the end of 1915, eighteen months before the explosion. Tunnels ran as deep as eighty feet, with hand pumps manned constantly to drain off the water that seeped in. The depth of the tunnels was necessary to provide safety against German countertunnels, *camouflets*, and vibration from the artillery shells flying into no-man's land at the surface. It was a massive engineering job, culminating in the planting of almost a million pounds of explosives.

The Germans detected the sound of deep digging, and sent trench raiding parties to steal some of the bags of earth that were being excavated. From soil samples, they determined the great depths at which the British were working. The Germans ignored the warning, believing that explosives planted so deeply could not possibly affect the surface fortifications and trenches.

At 3:10 on the morning of June 7, 1917, the 950,000 pounds of explosives were detonated simultaneously. The sound could be heard by Lloyd George at the prime minister's residence in London. A war correspondent who witnessed the explosion wrote:

> Out of the dark ridges of Messines and Wytschaete gushed enormous volumes of scarlet flame and of earth and smoke all lighted by the flame spilling over into fountains of fierce color, so that all the countryside was illuminated by red light. Where some of us stood watching, aghast and spellbound by this burning horror, the ground trembled and surged violently.

The Germans who survived clawed their way through tons of earth and wandered dazedly over the ground, which was bubbling from the heat generated by the explosion. Meeting little resistance, British, Irish, Australian, and New Zealand troops captured the ridge that same morning.

Haig wanted to mount a major offensive to capitalize on the advance, but civilian leadership, wary of offensives, withheld approval so that the follow-up attack did not get underway until July 20. By that time, the Germans had established new defensive positions.

The fighting that was to follow, known as the Third Battle of Ypres or the Battle of Passchendaele, was trench fighting at its worst. Passchendaele was actually only one phase of the five-month campaign, but the no-man's land there was so dreadful that the name stuck in the public mind.

The weather around Ypres was unfavorable for the British. There had been a dry spell in June and early July but by the time the attack began, the rains had come and the advance bogged down in mud.

Cautious because of the disaster at the Somme, the British confined themselves to limited objectives. These limited battles succeeded, at a cost that seemed moderate in manpower compared with that of the Somme. But the slowness of the advance was frustrating.

The mud became so thick that the British commanders thought the only way to advance quickly was by using the tanks. Headquarters of the tank corps warned that the armored vehicles would also bog down in the muddy conditions. Haig ignored these warnings, and disregarded the "swamp maps" that were prepared daily by tank officers. Haig's staff finally issued a memo asking them not to send any more maps. When tanks were sent through the muck and got stuck, the tank corps was blamed.

September was a dry month, and two limited offensives in September and a third in October brought the British closer to the town of Passchendaele. The rain began again. It fell almost continuously through the month of October and combined with the unceasing artillery barrages to destroy roads, trenches, forests, fields, and the town of Passchendaele itself.

It was during this battle that the Germans introduced mustard gas. Deceptive because it carried only a faint odor of horseradish and was virtually colorless, mustard gas acted on the skin rather than the lungs. Men attacked by mustard gas often didn't use their gas masks because they were unaware of the danger. On the skin, mustard gas could cause painful burns and blisters. One of the early victims at Ypres described its action on the eyes:

> I gave orders for all to put on their mouthpieces and noseclips so as to breathe none of the stuff and we carried on. Next morning myself and all of the 80 men were absolutely blind. One or two never recovered their sight and died.

The Germans had constructed a series of reinforced-concrete strongpoints called "pillboxes" and then broke the dikes in the area so that attackers would be unable to storm the strongpoints. The pillboxes were strong enough to withstand all but a direct hit by the artillery. From the safety of the pillboxes, German machine gunners blazed away at the British soldiers, who wallowed in a "porridge of mud."

Withdrawing all but the skeleton force manning the strongpoints, the Germans built six defensive lines in the rear, each with progressively stronger defenses. To penetrate these lines, British troops had to expose themselves to machine-gun fire from the pillboxes and enfilading fire from reinforcements drawn up from the rear trenches.

Unable to advance, the British responded with furious artillery fire, answered in kind by the Germans. They stirred up the "porridge" that by now engulfed the trench lines. Men, horses, and supply wagons sank without a trace in the mud.

Out in no-man's land, a British stretcher team struggles to bring in
a wounded soldier under enemy shellfire. NATIONAL ARCHIVES

Wounded Australian troops receiving medical attention in a dressing-station near the front during the Third Battle of Ypres. The man in the center is suffering from shell shock. AUSTRALIAN WAR MEMORIAL

The shrieks of men drowning in the mire affected the nerves of those who huddled under cover from the artillery barrages. Streams of mud collapsed the trench walls and buried men where they had fallen to sleep.

The shell craters from the artillery barrages were used as hiding places by troops whose trenches had been blasted out of existence. But the shell holes could be death traps. One man who survived Third Ypres described passing a crater in which he saw

> three heads in a row, the rest of the bodies submerged
> ... In another miniature pond, a hand still gripping
> a rifle is all that is visible, while its next-door neigh-
> bor is occupied by a steel helmet and half a head, the
> staring eyes staring icily at the green slime.

It became impossible to move through the muck; advances were measured in yards. Wheels of carts carrying artillery and supplies sank into the ground. It required twelve men just to carry a wounded man on a stretcher. They formed two lines, passing the stretcher forward while the men at the end made their way through the muck to the front of the parallel lines.

The wounded stuck rifles upright in the mud to call attention to themselves, but the stretcher bearers often never got to them and the rifles remained upright, after the men had bled to death, until artillery shells brought them down "like skittles," according to one observer.

Tanks were abandoned in the shell holes and in the burned-over woods around Passchendaele. Not a leaf remained—only the eerie blackened trunks that jutted upward through the mist and smoke that never seemed to lift.

When Haig's chief of staff visited the front for the first time, in November, he is said to have exclaimed, "Good God, did we really send men to fight in that?" and his guide said, "It's worse farther up."

Haig drove the attackers on and on, trying to take the high ground of Passchendaele before winter. He justified these attacks with his strategy of attrition—Falkenhayn's strategy at Verdun. In fact, the last advances of Canadian troops on Passchendaele Ridge only created a vulnerable salient that the German advance of the spring quickly crushed.

The grim joke spread through the lines that the war would end only when the last man on either side met face to face in a shell crater full of poisoned water and bodies. They would struggle for possession of the shell hole, and the victor, having killed the other man with his bare hands, would have won the war.

Soldiers kept each other's spirits up with talk of home. The "Blighty" of the British troops, the *Vaterland* of the Germans, and *la patrie* of the French were almost mythical places. The men thought of home as everything the trenches weren't: peaceful, clean, and decent. The thought of home was one of the things that kept the men in the trenches fighting.

As the war went on, seeming never to make any progress, conditions at home were changing. Men who left the trenches for leave at home found that it wasn't what they remembered at all.

At the beginning of the war, men motivated by duty and patriotism sprang at the opportunity to go to war. In Britain, which had a professional army, Lord Kitchener's call for the "first hundred thousand men" in August of 1914 brought 500,000 volunteers. France and Germany had raised huge armies through conscription, but there too the war was regarded as a sacred duty.

Not only the young burned with the idea of the war's nobility. Religious leaders, intellectuals, artists in each country trumpeted their belief in the rightness of the war. The bishop of London said it was the "greatest fight ever made for the Christian religion"; meanwhile, German soldiers' insignia proclaimed *Gott mit uns*—God is with us. Max Weber, a great German sociologist, wrote a friend, "This war, with all its

THE HOME FRONT 9

ghastliness, is nevertheless grand and wonderful. It is worth experiencing." The historian Werner Sombart wrote, "The war is holy, yes, the most sacred thing on earth."

Before the war some political parties on the left had pacifistic ideals. In the flush of patriotism after the declarations of war, however, all parties in all countries united in defense of the war effort.

Enthusiasm for the war was fanned by propaganda. Government-censored newspapers described as victories, pointless slaughters that gained tiny amounts of ground. People were told that victory would come soon.

Tales of the horrible actions of the Germans (the "Huns") as they marched through Belgium reached lurid and fantastic proportions. One story circulated about Germans hacking off and eating the hands of a Belgian baby. The Germans said the French gouged out the eyes of German prisoners in hospitals— a spy had seen the buckets of eyes. The French put out stories about German atrocities in the occupied regions of France— most of them untrue. But the press printed propaganda as fact. People had no other sources of information.

At the end of 1917, David Lloyd George, the British prime minister, remarked to a friend, "If people really knew, the war would be stopped tomorrow. But of course they don't know and can't know. The correspondents don't write and the censorship would not pass the truth."

The German army command held a press conference twice a week at which the war news was announced. The instructions of the officer who conducted the briefings included the reminder, "It is not so much the accuracy of news as its effect that matters."

The propaganda messages trapped the warring nations. Since the enemy was so evil, and since victory was near, a compromise peace was unacceptable. Throughout 1916 the two sides gingerly conducted negotiations for peace. But the Germans already occupied most of Belgium and large parts of France. They refused to retreat to their prewar boundaries, particularly since the British and French had secretly agreed to enrich their colonial empires at the expense of the Central Powers. Peace negotiations broke down because both sides had made such severe sacrifices of manpower. The politicians could not present their nations with a compromise peace, after so many lives had been sacrificed for total victory.

Recruitment propaganda was used to encourage more volunteers for the army. A French magazine showed a sketch of trench life—soldiers playing billiards, fencing, taking hot baths, and having a few convivial drinks together at the trench bar. Posed photographs showed men at the front obviously enjoying trench life. In Kensington Gardens in London, model trenches were set up for people to visit. They bore no resemblance at all to the rat-infested mudholes of Ypres and the Somme.

Despite propaganda the experience of total war was making itself felt at home. Newspapers printed casualty lists. Almost everyone read of a relative or neighbor who had been killed. The "Pals Battalions" decimated whole groups of young men whose friends and parents drew the conclusion that almost everyone who went to the war had been killed.

Trench warfare demanded an enormous amount of matériel. The French general staff estimated in 1914 that they would require 13,600 shells for their 75-millimeter guns every day. By September, 1915, they were demanding 150,000 75-millimeter shells daily.

It became necessary for the governments to exercise overall control of the economies of the nations at war. The military

Near the trench line in France, the home front could become a battle zone. Here the inhabitants of the town of Chalons sur Marne take refuge in a cave in 1918. LIBRARY OF CONGRESS

planners' belief in a short war had blinded them to the need for continuing sources of supplies. Previous wars could be fought by expanding certain sections of the economy or making other temporary arrangements within the existing system. For this war, the total economy of the nation had to be focused on winning. Changes in governmental structure, national economic planning, and social priorities were brought about by the national effort required to wage total war.

In France, a coalition of parties known as the *Union Sacrée* brought together politicians of every stripe, who submerged their feuds in the interests of national unity.

France suffered little from a shortage of food. In 1917, the French Ministry of Food ordered butchers to close two days a week, forbade the making of fancy cakes, and issued ration cards. Many Frenchmen, particularly those in the cities, lived as well as before. As in other countries at war, a "black market" in scarce goods flourished. The worst scarcity in France was coal because most of their coalfields were behind German lines. In winters people huddled together to conserve the little fuel available.

The French peasants and villagers living along the battle lines in northeast France suffered most. Many villages were obliterated by the shelling. Patrick MacGill writes of marching toward the front during the preparations for the Battle of Loos:

> Now and again, when a star-shell flamed over the firing line, we caught a glimpse of Bully-Grenay, huddled and helpless, its houses battered, its church riven, its chimneys fractured and lacerated. We dreaded passing the church; the cobbles on the roadway there were red with the blood of men.

A British soldier wrote home from France of crops unharvested in the fields because the men who had worked the farms were fighting or dead. Women and those too old or too young to fight tried to support their families by keeping up the farms. Some people opened *estaminets* to take advantage of the situation.

In Britain, the overall direction of the war was in the hands of the War Committee (later called the War Cabinet). At the beginning of the war, the War Committee included the Liberal government leadership plus representatives from the leading colonies and dominions of the empire. The empire nations contributed troops and economic aid to the war effort, and were granted a voice in the planning.

Britain's needs grew at a faster pace than France's or Germany's. The other two countries had already equipped large armies at the beginning of the war; Britain had to provide new equipment for the millions of new men it was placing under arms. In January, 1916, for the first time in its history, Britain turned to conscription. Since these new recruits were being taken away from industry at home, their loss was a double strain. Women took men's places in factories, farms, and offices, upsetting accepted ideas about their "proper" place.

Britain instituted a system of "voluntary" rationing. Each citizen was to be limited to four pounds of bread, two and a half pounds of meat, and three-quarters of a pound of sugar a week. This was lavish living compared to standards in Germany and the countryside of France.

Although some restrictions in Britain were voluntary, there was great social disapproval for those who violated them. Young women handed white feathers—a symbol of cowardice—to young men in the street who were in "mufti," or civilian clothes. Posters showing families at full tables of food bore the slogan: "Are you in league with the Kaiser?"

Germany went further than its two western-front opponents in organizing the economy for war. Walther Rathenau, a prominent businessman, was placed in charge of economic planning for the nation. Rathenau was given broad powers and exerted superhuman efforts to supply the enormous quantities of goods that Germany's soldiers on two fronts were consuming. He instituted a strict system of rationing of all necessary goods, and organized the nation's work force so that every available person would be where he or she was most needed for the war effort.

Germany's chemical industry was called upon to make synthetic materials to replace those they could no longer import due to the Allied blockade. They found substitutes for nitrates, essential for high explosives, for cotton, and other imports. The German word *ersatz*, meaning "substitute," became commonplace. Ersatz materials such as turnips and potatoes were used in the making of K (for *Krieg*, or war) bread. Coffee was made from acorns. Bandages were made from paper waste to preserve cotton. Other governments followed the models of planning instituted by Rathenau.

After the battles of the Somme and Verdun in 1916, attitudes on the home fronts changed. By now, the propagandists were unable to conceal the terrible costs of the war in lives and matériel. Resentment was widespread at the sacrifices of the war that were being made for no visible gains.

The sacrifices were great. Just in terms of money, the war was costing Britain $35 million a day. In Germany, the daily cost was $32 million by 1918. For the four years of the war, the budget of the French government came to 125 billion francs; normally it was 5 billion a year.

In Germany, the British blockade was increasingly effective. Despite Rathenau's efforts, millions felt the pinch of starvation. Germany retaliated with Zeppelin raids on London that killed hundreds, though the population failed to panic and demand peace, as the Germans hoped.

Outside Paris, the Germans brought in the greatest artillery weapon of the war. Called the Paris gun, it could fire an artillery shell into the heart of Paris, seventy-five miles away. At first, Parisians were not aware that the random explosions in the city were coming from a cannon. When the truth became known, Parisians simply accepted it as one more hardship of the war.

But French political unity at home began to dissolve. The Chamber of Deputies in secret sessions debated the meaning of Verdun. The newspapers did not even report the subject of the debate. Former Sergeant Maginot, who served at Verdun, began the debate by saying, "What might seem astonishing is that until now we have all kept quiet." The civilian leadership listened in shock to the stories of bloody, futile offensives repeated again and again.

In Britain, Prime Minister Herbert Asquith was replaced by a coalition government led by David Lloyd George. French governments rose and fell until in 1917 Georges Clemenceau formed a government that would lead France through the last year of the war. The people of Britain and France were demanding victory. Both Lloyd George and Clemenceau promised to deliver it. Clemenceau: "My foreign policy? I wage war. My domestic policy? I wage war. All the time I wage war."

In Germany in 1917, Chancellor Bethmann-Hollweg was dismissed. Hindenburg and Ludendorff were now running the country, overseeing all details of the conduct of the war, factory production, and distribution of food.

Other matters at home became more important than victory. Workers whose wages had been frozen for the duration of the war began to strike. Even munitions factories and war-related industries were hit with strikes.

In Germany, Socialists urged the workers to strike as a way of ending the war. On January 28, 1918, 400,000 workers in Berlin went on strike, demanding peace without annexation. Ludendorff put down the strike with harsh measures, but felt the pressure to bring a swift end to the war.

In 1917, in Britain and France, nearly 2 million working days were lost because of strikes. Wartime inflation and government attempts at controlling prices squeezed the middle class.

All three armies suffered in the field for lack of supplies, making the strikes harder to bear. Artillery shells had to be rationed: in some cases, gun crews were limited to six shells a day. The mass scale of the warfare had strained the resources of three of the mightiest nations in the world.

Reports of strikes at home disturbed the soldiers in the trenches. They compared their own wages with those of the strikers. In France, a factory worker earned 100 sous a day; the wages for soldiers were 5 sous a day. British soldiers earned a shilling a day; factory wages were much higher. In fact, the wages of empire troops like the Canadians were five shillings a day, and British troops felt cheated again when they saw the Canadians with more money in the *estaminets*.

When the soldiers came home on leave they were further disillusioned by what they saw. In Paris, on the surface, all was gaiety. Crowds filled the theaters to watch musical shows with patriotic themes. Popular singers learned the words to British and Canadian songs to please the empire soldiers who came there on furlough. Restaurants were filled. There were stories of war profiteers making millions from the war. A French doctor was convicted in a spectacular trial of selling medical discharges for several thousand francs each.

In London, farther from the battlefront, conditions were even stranger to the returning soldier. One officer wrote, "the only signs of war are that the men now wear short coats and black ties in the evenings, the dinners are shorter, and the servers fewer and less good."

Guy Chapman, a poet who served on the western front, recalled the London of that period as soldiers saw it.

> As the war trailed its body across France, sliming the landscape, so too it tainted civilian life. London seemed poorer and more raffish. Its dignity was melting under the strain. It had become corrupted . . . the good-timers, as the army abroad thought them, profiteering, drinking, debauching the women.

The soldiers reserved their greatest contempt for those who weren't aware of what was going on at the trenches. Siegfried Sassoon expressed it in a stanza:

> You smug-faced crowds with kindling eye
> Who cheer when soldier lads march by,
> Sneak home and pray you'll never know
> The hell where youth and laughter go.

Men found it impossible to share their experiences with their families and friends. The newspapers had given those at home an idea of the war that was too far removed from reality. Erich Maria Remarque expressed the feelings of many on returning home:

> My mother is the only one who asks no questions. Not so my father. He wants me to tell him about the front;

Letter writing helped link the soldiers to the home front. Here a French soldier writes a letter home in the midst of the wreckage of war. NATIONAL ARCHIVES

he is curious in a way that I find stupid and distressing . . . There is nothing he likes more than just hearing about it . . .

Returning to the front, the soldiers felt greater kinship with those men to whom they had to explain nothing, with those who had shared the trenches. A French soldier wrote of the alienation of the men who fought from those who did not: "We are divided into two foreign countries. The front . . . where there is too much misery, and the rear, where there is too much contentment."

Two events of 1917 far from the western trenches brought a decisive change in the war. One was the Russian Revolution; the other was the entry of the United States into the war on the side of the Allies. The Russian Revolution led to the Russians leaving the war, which meant that Germany could now concentrate all its efforts on the western front. On the other hand, the entry of the United States would bring fresh troops and supplies to the Allies.

The three opposing nations on the western front were exhausted. The French had barely made it through the year with their army intact. The British and Germans had drained each other at the Somme and Passchendaele. The Germans were feeling the pinch of the British blockade, and found themselves desperately short of supplies.

The Battle of Cambrai, launched on November 20, 1917, gave some hope to the British that the German trench defenses might be breachable after all. It was at Cambrai that tanks were used effectively for the first time.

This time, the advice of the tank commanders was followed. There were 324 tanks in the advance, massed together instead of scattered throughout a wide front. Instead of forewarning the enemy with a long preparatory bombardment, the tanks simply began moving forward as soon as the artillery fire began.

BREAKOUT 10

The tanks were backed up by infantry following close behind to consolidate the gains. Bundles of brush were brought along to fill the antitank trenches that the Germans had dug. Quickly, the British offensive gained about seven miles. But the British did not have enough troops to fully capitalize on the assault.

Cambrai was a small battle by World War I standards. In the end, it only produced a British salient that collapsed under a German counterattack. But the point had been made that under proper conditions the tanks could break the stalemate of the trenches.

Ludendorff was by now the effective ruler of Germany. He realized that if the Germans were to win, they would have to strike early and hard in the beginning of the year 1918, before the Americans arrived and before the Allies could amass more tanks. Ludendorff had reason to think a breakthrough was possible. On the eastern front in the previous year, two officers had made sizable gains using tactics that seemed to offer hope of success. The two men were General Oskar von Hutier and his chief of artillery, Colonel George von Bruchmuller, whose success had given him the nickname Durchbruchmuller. (*Durchbruch* means "breakthrough" in German.)

The Hutier tactics were those of infiltration. Instead of the normal procedure of massed frontal attacks against a broad trench line, the Hutier attacks "flowed like water," in Ludendorff's phrase, applying pressure on weak points in the line to break through. They were a development of the tactics used by the German troops in the early attacks on Verdun.

Ludendorff took the best soldiers from units on the eastern and western fronts and reorganized them in elite units for the early battles of 1918. These elite soldiers, known as "storm troops," led the attack by penetrating swiftly through the

German soldiers advancing as part of Ludendorff's gamble to win the war in 1918. The Germans made great gains, but decisive victory eluded them. LIBRARY OF CONGRESS

points of least resistance in the Allied line. Instead of advancing in a body across no-man's land, they were to infiltrate the front in small groups, inflicting casualties and worming their way behind the front line of defenses to attack the artillery in the rear.

Behind them came the storm battalions, which consisted of machine gunners, flamethrower units, and trench-mortar detachments. These were to strike at the fortified strongpoints that the storm troops had passed by, isolating and destroying them. Finally, the regular infantry would follow in mopping-up operations, consolidating the gains.

As head of the artillery, Bruchmuller contributed to the effectiveness of the German attacks by using elaborate combinations of shells. He laid down clouds of mustard gas to either side of the attacking force to keep Allied reinforcements from closing the gap. Bruchmuller combined high explosives, shrapnel, gas shells, smoke, and flares for maximum offensive effect. Use of air surveillance enabled Bruchmuller's artillery to zero in on the Allied strongpoints with greater accuracy than ever before in the war.

Meanwhile, the British were reconstructing their trench lines on the model of the German Hindenburg Line, building fortified strongpoints to hold the front line and more trenches in the rear to hold reserves.

The British deviated from the German plan in one important aspect, however: while the Germans had kept the front line very lightly manned and allotted only a third of their troops to the forward strongpoints, the British had more than two-thirds of their available forces in the strongpoints and the front lines. When the front lines proved vulnerable to the Hutier tactics, the British defense collapsed.

Ludendorff's chief objective was Flanders and the Ypres area.

He wanted to break through to the Channel ports that were supplying the British. However, bad weather would delay an effective offensive there until late in the year. Ludendorff decided to launch his first attack of 1918 in the Somme region, leaving the attack on Flanders until later.

The code name for the German offensive at the Somme was Operation Michael. Ludendorff envisioned a massive breakthrough to the city of Amiens. A major advance in this sector would separate the French and British armies.

Allied trench raids that took prisoners in the days before the attack gave some indication of the coming offensive. German prisoners seemed eager to be taken to the rear, indicating their fear of an artillery bombardment.

But the Allies could hardly have been prepared for the barrage that began early on March 21. It was the most intensive of the war, coming from six thousand German guns assembled along a forty-mile front from Arras to La Fère. It continued for four and a half hours, brief by the standards of World War I, but succeeded in destroying British communication lines, fortified strongpoints, and most of the trench system.

Weather helped the Germans. A heavy fog hung over the area, and the German storm troops were able to slip by the remaining British strongpoints and advance quickly across the trenches. The storm battalions knocked out the rest of the strongpoints. There was little for the following infantry to do but collect British prisoners and wreck the empty strongpoints. By the end of the first day, the Germans had made their greatest advance since 1914. They had made a bulge in the front fifty miles long and twenty-five miles deep.

But now Ludendorff made a critical mistake. His line had advanced unevenly. The storm troops had made their greatest advances in the southern part of the front where fog had been strongest. The troops moving toward Arras, in the north, had not made comparable advances. Ludendorff held back the units in the south so they would not become separated from the others. This critical delay gave the British enough time to regroup and bring in reinforcements. The Germans were never able to reach Amiens.

A factor in the slowness of the German advance was that the German soldiers were hungry. For a day, the road to Amiens lay open to them, but they were busy looting the food and clothing in the British billets and French towns along the way. A German officer described seeing

> men driving cows before them in a line; others who carried a hen under one arm and a box of notepaper under the other. Men carrying a bottle of wine under their arm and another one open in their hand . . . Men with top hats on their heads. Men staggering.

Operation Michael was not the decisive victory that Ludendorff envisioned. But the German advance alarmed the Allies so much that at last they agreed to some significant cooperation between their military forces. The French General Ferdinand Foch was charged with coordinating the French, British, and American armies on the western front. Essentially, Foch directed where reserves were to go, since the three army commanders, Pétain, Haig, and the American General John Pershing were adamant about maintaining some control of their men.

Meanwhile, Ludendorff was preparing to launch a second offensive, this time in Flanders, centering on the river Lys. The original plans were code-named St. George, but when the scope of the attack had to be scaled down because of lack of available troops, the offensive was renamed Georgette.

British soldiers surrendering to Germans. The setback caused by Ludendorff's sudden advances forced the Allies to unite under a single
commander—Marshal Foch. LIBRARY OF CONGRESS

The main objective of Georgette was the town of Hazebrouck, the center of railroad transport, communications, and supply for the entire northern part of the Allied trench line. If it fell to the Germans, the British would have problems supplying their troops in Flanders.

On April 7 and 8 a deluge of German mustard-gas shells fell on a twelve-mile front. On the ninth, Bruchmuller's "battering train"—the artillery battalions moved up from Operation Michael—arrived to join the bombardment. On the morning of the tenth, the German storm troops moved forward, again using Hutier's tactics to make substantial gains. Once again the Germans could not quite stretch the British line far enough, though they advanced to within five miles of Hazebrouck. Haig had shifted his forces to block the advance and Foch contributed five divisions from the precious reserve.

Ludendorff scanned the maps of the trenches, looking for a place where he could break the line. He decided again on a place which had already seen heavy bloodshed. The next German offensive, Operation Blucher, would thrust at the Chemin des Dames Ridge between La Fère and Reims.

It was an inviting place for the German attack: the French commanding general in that sector had failed to obey Pétain's orders to increase the depth and flexibility of his trench system. He still kept most of his infantry in the front-line trenches and he had made little effort to reinforce the trenches and dugouts so that they could withstand the German artillery.

German artillery began another intense bombardment on May 27 along the Chemin des Dames Ridge. A gas attack was followed by shrapnel shells that inflicted many casualties on the French soldiers grouped in the shallow frontline trenches. German storm troops reached their immediate objective, the Vesle River, by that evening. On May 30, the Germans advanced to the Marne and seemed once more to be threatening Paris.

But in fact Ludendorff had reached the end of his resources. Once again the Allied line bent but did not break. The German advance slowed under pressure from Allied reinforcements.

Among these reinforcements were units of the American Third Division, who met the Germans on June 2 at the town of Château-Thierry. Beyond Château-Thierry, the road was open to Paris. The Americans successfully defended the road west of the town, driving the Germans back. Their success cheered the French troops fighting alongside.

More encouraging was an American counterattack on June 6, which had as its objective the German-held Belleau Wood. The Americans advanced in the same open formations that the British had used early in the war. German machine-gun fire drove them back time and time again. By June 25, after suffering heavy casualties but continuing to advance tenaciously, the Americans prevailed and took Belleau Wood. The Germans nicknamed the Americans *teufelhunden,* or devil dogs. Ominously for Ludendorff, 300,000 more American soldiers were arriving in France every month.

Ludendorff's desperate gamble had failed. The trench stalemate had been broken, but now the Germans occupied vulnerable salients requiring great numbers of men to defend and without the heavy fortifications of the Hindenburg Line. Furthermore, Ludendorff had sacrificed the best part of his army with the Hutier storm-troop tactics. He had no more good replacements.

For the next two months the Germans continued to attack in the south, trying to straighten the salients in their advance. These attacks gained little new ground, and at the beginning of July, Ludendorff turned once again to Flanders. He planned a thrust toward Reims to draw Allied troops from Flanders so that the Germans could finally break through the British lines there. Ludendorff was in the Flanders area, preparing to direct the operations personally, when word reached him that the Allies had launched a major counterattack at the Marne.

General Charles Mangin directed an Allied army composed of French, British, and American divisions that carried the thrust of the attack at the Marne. Three other French armies also participated. The offensive was spearheaded by 350 tanks, which broke through the German lines. Quickly the infantry followed, crushing the German salient back to the Vesle River.

Following up this success, Foch, now coordinating all the troops on the western front, planned more counterattacks against the vulnerable German salients. The British, strengthened with new reinforcements from home, launched an attack near Amiens on August 8. Again massed tanks were used to lead the way.

This time the German army cracked. The Allies captured thirty thousand German prisoners and five hundred guns. Whole German divisions simply threw down their arms and surrendered. German reinforcements sent to shore up the line were mocked by retreating soldiers, who shouted, "You're prolonging the war." Ludendorff wrote in his diary that August 8 was "the black day of the German army." He feared he had reached the end.

But the old problems of trench warfare reasserted themselves, and the British found themselves unable to deliver the knockout blow. They could not send reinforcements through the line quickly enough to keep the offensive going. Motorized troop transport was still not available in strength, and the tanks simply outran the army.

With the counteroffensives ordered by Foch, The Allies threw the Germans on the defensive again. Here British soldiers discover a German straggler. BETTMAN ARCHIVE

The Germans now began a long retreat. They fell back to the Hindenburg Line, where they still were able to maintain a strong defensive position against attacks. In other areas, the two armies now fought in improvised trenches that were little more than huge shell craters tied together with short trenches. The Germans were not routed, and the war went on.

In the south at the St. Mihiel salient, which the Germans had held since 1914, American divisions and one French corps, led by tanks and a creeping artillery barrage, pressed forward. In four days, from September 12 to 16, they crushed the salient, advancing as much as thirteen miles. At the request of Foch, Pershing then shifted his forces north to participate in the Meuse-Argonne offensive.

Although the war had broken out into a war of movement on some sectors, in the Meuse-Argonne the trench lines were still stationary. The Americans, unfortunately, had not learned from the lessons of earlier battles on the western front. They launched senseless and costly attacks similar to the earlier Allied and German offensives. The heavily wooded area known as the Argonne Forest also slowed the American advance. It was not until the end of October that the Argonne was cleared of Germans, and at the time of the Armistice the campaign was still going on. More American lives were lost at the Meuse-Argonne than in any other battle in United States history.

On September 26, Foch threw 160 Allied divisions into the fighting all along the front in a general offensive designed to finish the war at last. He had another 60 divisions in reserve. To hold back the Allies, the Germans had 197 divisions in all, but Allied intelligence rated only 51 of them as effective fighting units.

Even with this overpowering force, Foch was not able to

American troops in a shallow trench in the Meuse valley. The camouflage was left by Germans retreating to another position across the river. NATIONAL ARCHIVES

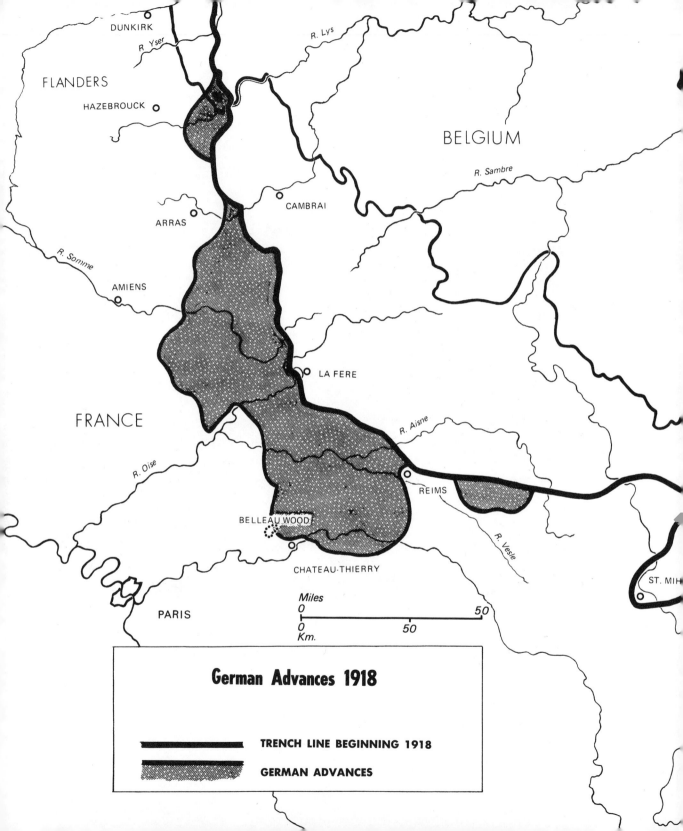

DUNKIRK

R. Yser

R. Lys

FLANDERS

HAZEBROUCK

BELGIUM

R. Sambre

CAMBRAI

ARRAS

R. Somme

AMIENS

LA FERE

FRANCE

R. Aisne

R. Oise

REIMS

BELLEAU WOOD

R. Vesle

CHATEAU-THIERRY

ST. MIH

PARIS

Miles
0   50
0   50
Km.

German Advances 1918

TRENCH LINE BEGINNING 1918

GERMAN ADVANCES

make a decisive breakthrough. Although their successes continued, the Allies ran into the same problems that had plagued the Germans in 1914. The farther they got from their sources of supply, the slower they advanced. Communications were never good, and motorized vehicles never plentiful enough to supply a fast-moving advance.

The number of tanks available to the Allies was still too small for a breakthrough on a wide front, and the tanks were still dependent on the infantry to follow up and consolidate gains. The retreating Germans left machine gunners in heavily fortified positions to hold up the advancing armies.

In southern Europe, the Allied troops that had been bottled up in Salonika for so long broke out and moved against Germany's allies. Austria-Hungary, which had managed to continue the war only with German help, was crumbling. Soon Germany would have to defend itself from the east as well.

On September 29 Ludendorff asked the civilian government to begin negotiations for an armistice. In October, however, Ludendorff seemed to have a renewal of spirit. He began to make plans for a new defensive line from which to continue the fighting.

But it was too late. Rumors of the impending defeat affected the German army, who had seen their promised victory offensives smashed. Some of the troops were starving; all were exhausted after four years of brutal trench fighting. They could not have gone on; replacements were arriving who were fourteen years old and younger.

Erich Maria Remarque wrote what the German soldier was thinking then:

> Never was life in the line more bitter and more full
> of horror than in the hours of the bombardment, when
> the blanched faces lie in the dirt, and the hands

An American gun crew firing against German positions during the
Meuse-Argonne offensive. NATIONAL ARCHIVES

clutch at the one thought: No! No! Not now! Not now at the last moment!

An armistice was negotiated, to go into effect on the eleventh hour of the eleventh day of the eleventh month. The guns stopped on the western front at last. The war was over.

When the Armistice came, the cheering was heartfelt, but it had none of the elation that had greeted the declarations of war more than four years earlier. The dominant feeling was relief—relief that the killing had stopped, relief at being alive to cheer when so many others were not.

The casualties were enormous, the total of four years of horror. Counting only deaths, Great Britain had lost 761,000, the French 1,358,000, and the Germans something like 2,000,000 on all fronts. But not even these chilling figures indicate the extent of the loss. For the survivors were not evenly distributed among the population. The war spared the old, the very young, and most of the women. Many felt it spared the shirker at the expense of the more courageous.

By the end of the war, the ranks of the young men of Europe were decimated. Between the years 1914 and 1918, France lost 20 percent of its men between twenty and forty-four, Germany 15 percent, and Great Britain 10 percent. For both France and Britain, these figures were higher than those for World War II.

World War I had struck down the rising generation, those who had been most daring, most intelligent, and most endowed with the qualities of leadership. The most promising youth had often been first to volunteer in Britain, chosen as line-officer

DISILLUSIONMENT 11

candidates in Britain and France, and selected to be among Ludendorff's storm troops. They were the ones most likely to have been killed.

And these figures give only the dead. Many, many more were wounded. Millions lost arms or legs, were blinded or incapacitated by gas, had their bodies shattered by exploding shells, or their minds shattered by strain. Their lives were ruined.

The physical damage to the war-torn areas of Belgium and northern France was enormous, and there was no money to pay for postwar restoration. World War I had been the most expensive war in history. The countries of Europe had poured out their accumulated treasure and the treasures of their empires to finance it. Before 1914, they had been creditors to the world; now, they were debtor nations.

Where the trench line had snaked its way through Europe, devastation was complete. Some villages were completely obliterated. Land that once was fertile now was barren, poisoned soil. Some villagers returned and attempted to rebuild the towns as they had been before the war. To do this, the trench system had to be filled in. Unexploded shells and unburied bodies made the task a grisly one.

Britain helped in this endeavor in the Somme region. British villages whose "Pals" battalions had suffered great casualties in a certain area of the front adopted these areas and contributed to the restoration. It was a long process and some of it was never completed.

In the battle areas, at least the damage could be seen and work begun. In the larger postwar society, the damage was less easily identified. The war made its effect felt on the victors as well as the defeated for years afterward.

The British were to be timid in the years following the war

and were to follow a policy of appeasement in the face of an emerging, aggressive Germany in the 1930s. The terrible price of World War I made another war unthinkable for them.

The French too were scarred emotionally. The lesson they learned from World War I was the wrong one. The spirit of attack was totally discredited. The French were to adopt the stalemate of the trenches as a national policy and spirit of defense, even after the new weapons and tactics combined with greater mechanization to make the offensive powerful once again. They were to hide behind the Maginot Line in the face of a new German threat.

The Germans had had no devastation in their homeland, but reparations forced on them by the peace treaty crippled them economically. The psychological torment of defeat contributed to the rise of Nazism. World War II would be to some degree Germany's attempt to wipe out the defeat of World War I.

The soldiers who returned home alive faced a bleak future. The French soldiers came back to a dispirited nation, and often to villages that had been erased or were ghostly images of what they had been before. Like all the other soldiers, they returned to economic hard times.

Britain's prime minister, Lloyd George, had made a pledge to the fighting men during the war. They would return, he said, to a "home fit for heroes," a phrase that would haunt him. These returning heroes often could not find jobs. Those who had fought in the trenches resented those who had sat out the war and were doing well. The government could not provide adequate pensions, job programs, or education for them. One soldier recalled those postwar days:

> More than anything I hated to see war-crippled men
> standing in the gutter selling matches. We had been

promised a land fit for heroes; it took a hero to live in it. I'd never fight for my country again.

In Germany, the transition was even more difficult. The demobilized soldiers often wandered without purpose, finding it difficult to find a place in the shattered society. Veterans found solace in groups of other war veterans. They formed the core of paramilitary organizations like the *Freikorps* that often rallied behind extremist reactionary movements. Violence in the streets seemed tame to those who had experienced the violence of the trenches. The ultimate violence of Hitler's Reich was but a step further.

It was psychologically difficult for the demobilized soldiers to readjust to peace after life in the trenches. The trenches had made extreme demands on the fighting men. They had lived on the edge of death for what seemed like an interminable period. Many had recurrent nightmares of the horrors they had seen. Many remembered the physical and psychological preparation for facing death, the tension caused by the need to be constantly alert. These extreme emotions did not disappear when they entered civilian life. Remarque, anticipating this state of mind, wrote:

> And this I know: all these things that now, while we are still in the war, sink down in us like a stone, after the war shall waken again, and then shall begin the disentanglement of life and death.

Four years of war had transformed Europe's ideals. The fervent patriotism of the prewar years, which sounds simpleminded to us sixty years later, was idealism, strongly felt, believed in, and acted on in World War I. The nature of patriotism changed. Knowledge of the horrors of modern warfare removed romanticism and heroism from war. Fighting because your country called you, which was a cherished duty in 1914, became a job to be done in 1940. Ford Madox Ford summed up the death of this kind of patriotism in a postwar novel:

No more Hope, no more Glory, no more parades for you and me any more. Nor for the country . . . Nor for the world, I dare say . . . None . . . Gone . . . Napoo finny!

No . . . more . . . parades!

Along with patriotism went many of the other old values that the pre-1914 world had felt were eternal. In the trenches fair play and honesty did not ensure survival. A toughening of outlook and a cynicism were products of the horrors of the western front.

The old class biases were also weakened. In the trenches there was a rough equality based on sharing the imminence of death. The returning soldiers did not want to go back to the more rigidly class-oriented society of pre-1914. Nor could their officers act as confidently as if their social position qualified them to lead those of lesser station. Society, schooling, and birth had traditionally kept them distant from the men with whom they shared the trenches. In their shared agony, class differences dropped away and could not be put back.

Those who had served in the war became known as the "lost generation." The brotherhood of the trenches was deep and real. Based on an unspeakable suffering, it marked for life those who served and set them apart from others who had not served. The alienation between the trenches and the home front was never to be healed.

Remarque again spoke for the men of that generation:

And men will not understand us.... We will be superfluous even to ourselves, we will grow older, a few will adapt themselves, some others will merely submit, and most will be bewildered—the years will pass by and in the end we shall all fall into ruin.

These are some of the books we consulted in writing this book. If you are interested in World War I, many of them are worth looking up in your local library. Some are available in paperback. There were many personal accounts of war experiences written from 1916 onward. Unfortunately, most of these are out of print, but your library may have them.

Aron, Raymond, *The Century of Total War,* Boston, Beacon Press, 1954.

One of the most thought-provoking books written on our century. It traces the effect of the "total war" of World War I through the postwar period after World War II. It shows how the demands of World War I on the participating countries contributed to later events in the postwar world.

Barbusse, Henri, *Under Fire,* New York, E. P. Dutton, 1917.

A novel written during the war that shows life in the trenches from the viewpoint of the French *poilus.* It emphasizes the horrors and dehumanization of the war.

Carrington, Charles, *Soldier from the Wars Returning,* New York, David McKay, 1965.

An account of World War I from the point of view of a man who served as a young British officer.

FOR FURTHER READING

Chapman, Guy, *A Passionate Prodigality,* New York, Holt, Rinehart, and Winston, 1966.

One of the best accounts of trench warfare, written by a man who served as a British officer.

Ellis, John, *Eye-Deep in Hell,* New York, Pantheon Books, 1976.

An account of trench warfare on the western front with emphasis on the British participation. Includes many excerpts from eyewitness accounts.

Ellis, John, *The Social History of the Machine Gun,* New York, Pantheon Books, 1975.

A history of the machine gun with implications for modern war from its development in the second part of the nineteenth century to the period after World War I.

Empey, Arthur Guy, *Over the Top,* New York, G. P. Putnam's Sons, 1917.

A lively account of the experiences of an American who enlisted in the British army in 1915. Excellent source of information on the daily life of soldiers in the trenches.

Falls, Cyril, *The Great War 1914–1918,* New York, Capricorn Books, 1959.

A fine short history of the war by a British historian.

Fitzsimons, Bernard, ed., *Tanks and Weapons of World War I,* Sydney, Ure Smith, 1973.

Good information on the importance of weapons on World War I with first-person accounts of their use by all sides.

Ford, Ford Madox, *No More Parades,* New York, New American Library, 1964.

A series of four novels set in England before, during, and after the war.

Fussell, Paul, *The Great War and Modern Memory,* New York, Oxford University Press, 1975.

The war and its effect on modern literature, with emphasis on the experience of the trenches.

Graves, Robert, *Good-Bye to All That,* Garden City, N.Y., Doubleday Anchor Books, 1929, 1975.

An autobiographical account by the famous poet. Includes his experiences as a British officer in the trenches.

Hogg, Ian V., *The Guns 1914–1918,* New York, Ballantine Books, 1971.

A good, short, authoritative account of the artillery of World War I by a British expert.

Horne, Alistair, *The Price of Glory,* New York, St. Martin's Press, 1963.

A fine account of the Battle of Verdun, stressing the strategy and character of the leaders involved as well as the tremendous human cost of the struggle.

Houlihan, Michael, *World War I Trench Warfare,* London, Ward Lock Ltd., 1974.

Trench warfare from the viewpoint of the British. Fine pictures and diagrams.

Keegan, John, *The Face of Battle,* New York, Viking Press, 1976.

Asks what makes men act as they do during a battle. One of the three classic battles considered is the Somme.

Keegan, John, *Opening Moves: August 1914,* New York, Ballantine Books, 1971.

An excellent, concise book on the history of the first month of the war.

King, Jere Clemens, ed., *The First World War,* New York, Walker and Company, 1972.

Selections of writings on the various phases of the war. Many firsthand accounts.

Knightley, Phillip, *The First Casualty,* New York, Harcourt Brace Jovanovich, 1975.

An account of how newspapers have covered wars since the mid-nineteenth century. Includes the effect of propaganda on war reportage.

Liddell Hart, B. H., *The Real War, 1914–1918,* Boston, Little, Brown, 1964.

First-rate short account of the war. Captain Liddell Hart not only served in the war but is an eminent historian.

Lloyd, Allan, *The War in the Trenches,* London, Hart-Davis, MacGibbon, 1976.

War in the trenches during World War I told from the British viewpoint with excerpts from eyewitness accounts of battles and living conditions.

MacGill, Patrick, *The Great Push,* New York, Grosset and Dunlap, 1916.

An eyewitness account of the Battle of Loos and other action on the western front during 1915.

Marshall, S. L. A., *World War I,* New York, American Heritage Press, 1971.

A concise, clear, and lively account of the war by a superb military historian.

Messenger, Charles, *Trench Fighting 1914–1918,* New York, Ballantine Books, 1972.

Excellent account of trench fighting on the western front

with emphasis on how it evolved from battle to battle throughout the war.

Middlebrook, Martin, *The First Day on the Somme,* New York, W. W. Norton and Company, 1972.

A fascinating reconstruction of the first day of the Battle of the Somme by a man who interviewed survivors half a century later. Much of the book is told in the words of the participants.

Morris, Eric; Johnson, Curt; Chant, Christopher; Willmott, H.P., *Weapons and Warfare of the 20th Century,* London, Octopus Books, 1975.

Survey of weapons of the twentieth century with excellent drawings and technical information.

Remarque, Erich Maria, *All Quiet on the Western Front,* Greenwich, Conn., Fawcett, 1961.

Classic German novel of the war written by a man who served.

Sassoon, Siegfried, *Memoirs of an Infantry Officer,* New York, Coward-McCann, 1930.

Poignant novel of the war written by a British poet who served.

Taylor, A. J. P., *The First World War,* New York, Capricorn Books, 1972.

A good general account of the war by one of the eminent historians of Great Britain.

Taylor, A. J. P., ed., *History of World War I,* London, Octopus Books, 1974.

Articles by many contributors on all phases of the war.

Tuchman, Barbara W. *The Guns of August,* New York, Bantam Books, 1976.

A classic account of the outbreak of war and the opening battles.

Watt, Richard, *Dare Call It Treason,* London, Chatto and Windus, 1964.

A fine account of the French mutinies of 1917 and the political and military situation of France during the war.

Witkop, Philipp, ed., *German Students' War Letters,* New York, E. P. Dutton.

Collection of letters written by German students serving in the German army during the war.

Wren, Jack, *The Great Battles of World War I,* New York, Castle Books, 1971.

A lively account of the major battles of the war, with superb illustrations.

INDEX

Grateful acknowledgment is made to the following for permission to quote material:

From *Over the Top,* by Arthur Guy Empey, Copyright 1917 by Arthur Guy Empey. Reprinted by permission of the publisher, G. P. Putnam's Sons.

From *Under Fire* by Henri Barbusse, Copyright renewal, 1947, by J. M. Dent. Reprinted by permission of the publishers, E. P. Dutton.

G. T. Sassoon and The Viking Press, Inc., for "Suicide in Trenches" from *Collected Poems* by Siegfried Sassoon, copyright 1918 by E. P. Dutton and Co., copyright renewed 1946 by Siegfried Sassoon.

Doubleday & Co. for *The Great Push,* by Patrick MacGill, Copyright 1916, by George H. Doran Company.

All maps by Larry Sicking

THE AUTHORS

Dorothy Law Hoobler received her master's degree in history from New York University and has been a free-lance writer and editor for several years. She and her husband, Thomas Hoobler, live in New York City and have a young daughter. They are the authors of the well-received *Photographing History: The Career of Mathew Brady* from Putnam's.

Thomas Hoobler graduated from the University of Notre Dame with a degree in English and studied at the Writer's Workshop of the University of Iowa under Kurt Vonnegut. With his wife, Dorothy, he is the coauthor of eleven books.